'It is not always easy to understand wh[...] syndrome. Comprehensive and acces[...] the key clinical features, managemen[...] to day-to-day life. The authors have aone a great job in putting together a highly useful resource for patients and their families, as well as professionals and teachers dealing with this condition in the school setting.'

– Andrea E. Cavanna, MD PhD FRCP,
Consultant in Behavioural Neurology

'Uttom Chowdhury and Tara Murphy have been committed for years to the care of children and families affected by Tourette syndrome and have trained many other clinicians. This book combines the medical literature with their experience of the condition, its challenges and its treatment, including in the home and classroom. It will be a valuable resource for both parents and professionals.'

– Dr Jeremy Stern, Consultant Neurologist and
Honorary Medical Director, Tourettes Action

'This accessible book from experienced clinicians helps families live with and accept tics. At the same time it provides guidance to enable parents to make the best use of professional advice and expect a high standard of assessment and treatment for their child. It acknowledges and explains the neurological basis of tics and Tourette's but avoids excessive preoccupation with the unusual symptoms. It also gently dismisses the myth that doctors have a full answer to tics and Tourette's. Instead the emphasis is on families learning to identify and access the help they need. Part of this process is realising that their child's difficulties may not be the tics themselves, but a related problem such as anxiety or learning difficulties. There are practical tips for families throughout – with the repeated message that "knowledge is power".'

– Professor Isobel Heyman, Clinical Lead, National Tourette
Syndrome Clinic, Great Ormond Street Hospital, London

Why Do You Do That?
A Book about Tourette Syndrome for Children and Young People
Uttom Chowdhury and Mary Robertson
Illustrated by Liz Whallett
ISBN 978 1 84310 395 0
eISBN 978 1 84642 491 5

Disorganized Children
A Guide for Parents and Professionals
Edited by Samuel M. Stein and Uttom Chowdhury
ISBN 978 1 84310 148 2
eISBN 978 1 84642 496 0

Can I tell you about Tourette Syndrome?
A guide for friends, family and professionals
Mal Leicester
Illustrated by Apsley
ISBN 978 1 84905 407 2
eISBN 978 0 85700 806 0
Part of the Can I tell you about…? series

Kids in the Syndrome Mix of ADHD, LD, Autism
Spectrum, Tourette's, Anxiety, and More!
The one-stop guide for parents, teachers, and other professionals
Martin L. Kutscher, MD
With contributions from Tony Attwood, PhD and Robert R. Wolff, MD
ISBN 978 1 84905 967 1
eISBN 978 0 85700 882 4

The Parent's Guide to Specific Learning Difficulties
Information, Advice and Practical Tips
Veronica Bidwell
ISBN 978 1 78592 040 0
eISBN 978 1 78450 308 6

PANDAS and PANS in School Settings
A Handbook for Educators
Edited by Patricia Rice Doran
ISBN 978 1 84905 744 8
eISBN 978 1 78450 166 2

TIC DISORDERS

A Guide for Parents and Professionals

UTTOM CHOWDHURY AND TARA MURPHY

FOREWORD BY SUZANNE DOBSON
CHIEF EXECUTIVE OF TOURETTES ACTION UK

Jessica Kingsley *Publishers*
London and Philadelphia

First published in 2017
by Jessica Kingsley Publishers
73 Collier Street
London N1 9BE, UK
and
400 Market Street, Suite 400
Philadelphia, PA 19106, USA

www.jkp.com

Library of Congress Cataloging in Publication Data
Names: Chowdhury, Uttom, 1967- author. | Murphy, Tara, 1976- author.
Title: Tic disorders : a guide for parents and professionals / Uttom
   Chowdhury and Tara Murphy ; foreword by Suzanne Dobson.
Description: London ; Philadelphia : Jessica Kingsley Publishers, 2017. |
   Includes bibliographical references and index.
Identifiers: LCCN 2016019281 | ISBN 9781849050616
Subjects: LCSH: Tourette syndrome in children--Popular works. | Tic
   disorders--Popular works.
Classification: LCC RJ496.T68 C472 2017 | DDC 618.92/83--dc23 LC record
available at https://urldefense.proofpoint.com/v2/url?u=https-3A__lccn.loc.
gov_2016019281&d=BQIFAg&c=euGZstcaTDllvimEN8b7jXrwqOf-v5A_
CdpgnVfiiMM&r=VCKr2NBFNTs4O_kp07esGY2J-doQEb4zTq5sCaeXa-
I&m=ifP7-ROy6p1CpfWa41fzyzvq5ixvRc6-TZ7OOij0VfQ&s=91cao7lt-IPCfN
MocMJIQf6yyz94M5tdMO7R3ls2y30&e=

British Library Cataloguing in Publication Data
A CIP catalogue record for this book is available from the British Library

ISBN 978 1 84905 061 6
eISBN 978 0 85700 917 3

Printed and bound in Great Britain

For Ruth, Sacha, Max and Mia.
For Linda and Patrick Murphy.

Contents

Acknowledgements

I would like to thank all the children and parents I have met in various clinics and support groups over the last 20 years. I have learnt, and continue to learn, so much from working alongside the families I have met.

Uttom Chowdhury
April 2016

I wish to thank Kate McCullagh and Zeeniya Bryan, parents who kindly reviewed an earlier version of this book, and gave enormously helpful feedback.

I am also grateful to Suzanne Dobson for reviewing the text and also Tourettes Action for supporting the development and dissemination of behavioural treatments for tic disorders (amongst other areas) here in the UK. Although there is still much work to do, we have come a long way.

I am keen to acknowledge my colleagues in the scientific community for collaboration but also for moving forward with a better informed understanding of Tourette syndrome – from these colleagues I gain understanding and confidence. I am indebted to our team at Great Ormond Street Hospital and in particular my friend and colleague Professor Isobel Heyman, Consultant Child Psychiatrist, from whom I have learnt and continue to learn a great deal. However, the main inspiration for the book came from the children and their families at the Tourette syndrome clinic at Great Ormond Street Hospital NHS Foundation Trust who have taught me so much and make it all worthwhile.

Finally, I am indebted to my husband, Damon Millar, who gives me inspiration, love and a sense of what can be.

Tara Murphy
April 2016

Foreword

I was delighted when Tara and Uttom decided to write this book and even more delighted to be asked to write a few words by way of introduction.

Tics and Tourette syndrome (TS) are perhaps the most difficult of the neurological conditions to understand. Their strange and constantly changing nature causes more misunderstanding amongst the general public and the beleaguered GP than anything else, and this leads to an increase in fear and stigma and a lack of treatment, which just adds to the difficulties of people living with the syndrome. From our helpline at Tourettes Action we know that there are three main stages to understanding TS. First, parents tell us, they begin to notice that their child is not doing the same as his peers at about five years of age; for a while they worry and try to help their child not do these strange things; then they worry some more and begin to search the internet: could it be? Surely not – but maybe. Second, the parents might phone the Tourettes Action helpline where someone will explain the symptoms and criteria and offer to send a list of specialists in Tourette. We suggest a visit to their GP to ask his opinion and for a referral to a specialist. It is at this, the third stage, that there is sometimes a slight hiccup; the GP may say, 'It's not TS – he isn't swearing.' It is hoped, however, that the child is referred to a specialist who can advise the family, who can then begin the journey of acceptance and management.

This excellent book will soon dispel that myth and many others about TS. It gives clear guidance about what the syndrome is, how it presents and who should be contacted for a firm diagnosis.

To get a diagnosis, to understand what is happening to your child or in rarer circumstance your teenager or an adult, is both a huge relief and the beginning of a bewildering journey. As you will learn, there is no particular medication for TS; there is a wealth of medication that will moderate symptoms and maybe help, but as you will also learn, these are not without side effects. Should you choose not to medicate your child (or yourself) that seems to be the end of it apart from maybe a follow-up appointment in a year. This is where the book comes into its own, discussing the pros and cons of medication and, importantly, the psychological therapies, giving you a better understanding and certainty about what is right for you and perhaps the ability to guide your patient through the maze.

Tourette syndrome is rarely alone and in this book you will learn about the other conditions that are often seen with TS, understand them, and maybe begin to see some solutions for you.

When I first read a draft of this book I wondered why such a publication did not already exist. Here in one volume, written in an accessible manner, by people who have spent a huge amount of their professional lives working with those living with Tourette syndrome, is everything you need to know to at least gain a good working knowledge and understanding of TS. This knowledge will be hugely important for health professionals and people caring for someone who lives with TS. I am so pleased that such a volume exists and hope it will soon be on not only every worried parent's reading list but also those of GPs and those charged with supporting someone with TS.

Suzanne Dobson
Chief Executive of Tourettes Action UK

Part 1

Tics and Tourette Syndrome

1

What Are Tic Disorders?

The main characteristic of any tic disorder is an involuntary rapid recurrent non-rhythmic movement or sound. Tics that produce movement are called 'motor tics', while tics that produce sound are called 'vocal tics'. Tics are sudden and purposeless. At one end of the spectrum of tic disorders are children with brief episodes of single motor or vocal tics. At the other end of the spectrum are children with chronic multiple tics, which is typically referred to as Tourette syndrome. Tourette syndrome is defined as the individual having multiple motor and at least one vocal tic, which continue for a year or more but probably change with time. This spectrum of conditions is presented below in Figure 1.1.

| transient tic disorder | chronic tic disorder | mild tourette syndrome | severe tourette syndrome |

Figure 1.1 Tic disorder spectrum

For descriptive purposes, tics can be divided into simple tics and complex tics. Simple motor tics are fast and meaningless, and include eye blinking, grimacing and shoulder shrugging. Complex motor tics tend to be slower, involve several muscle groups and may appear to be purposeful; they include hopping, kissing, touching objects, echopraxia (imitating the movement of other people) and copropraxia (obscene gestures). Simple vocal tics may involve sniffing, coughing, clearing one's throat and whistling; complex vocal tics include the repetition of certain words or phrases such as 'You know', 'Yeah, yeah, yeah' or 'All right' with the phrase being repeated until it feels just right. Other complex vocal tics include differences in the articulation of speech, for example, variations in the rhythm, tone and rate of a sentence or sentences. The most widely known but quite rarely experienced form of vocal tic is referred to as coprolalia and describes the repetitive use of obscene or socially unacceptable words or phrases. Tics can occur in nearly any part of the body; Table 1.1 gives a detailed description of the diversity of the most common tics.

Table 1.1 Common motor and vocal tics

	Motor tics	Vocal tics
Simple	Eye blinking Grimacing Lip pouting Head turning Shoulder shrugging Frowning Limb jerking Abdominal tensing	Clearing throat Coughing Sniffing Whistling Hissing Grunting Animal sounds
Complex	Hopping Clapping Squatting Touching objects Kissing Picking at clothing Copropraxia Echopraxia	Repeating words or phrases Unusual rhythms, tone or volume Mimicking accents Coprolalia

Transient tic disorder

With transient tic disorder, tics only last a few weeks or months and are usually confined to the face and neck, although body location may vary. Motor tics are most common but sometimes vocal tics can be experienced. Transient tic disorders are also called 'provisional tic disorder' under the new classification system in the DSM-5 (American Psychiatric Association 2013).

The age of onset is usually three to ten years, with more boys being affected than girls. Although transient tics do not, by definition, persist for more than a year, it is not uncommon for a child to have a series of transient tics over the course of several years. Transient tic disorder is very common and some studies have even suggested that up to 18 per cent of children under ten years of age will experience some period of tics. This form of tic rarely bothers the child and for many youngsters will go unnoticed.

Chronic motor or vocal tic disorder

Chronic tic disorders include blinking, sniffing or neck movements which occur for more than a year and, unlike transient tics, tend to persist with the same tic. Community surveys indicate that between 1 per cent and 3 per cent of children manifest some form of chronic tic (Scharf *et al.* 2012).

Tourette syndrome (combined multiple motor and vocal tics)

The most severe type of tic disorder is called Tourette syndrome. The label is attributed to a French neurologist, Georges Albert Édouard Brutus Gilles de la Tourette, who worked at the Salpêtrière Hospital, Paris, France, in the 19th century (Robertson 2015). The diagnostic criteria for

Tourette syndrome is that the individual has had multiple motor tics and one or more vocal tics present at some time, but not necessarily concurrently. The tics may occur many times a day, and sometimes nearly every day.

The onset is usually during childhood before the age of 18 years. Tics usually start at about six years of age but can start much earlier in some children. Typically, motor types are experienced first and then vocalisations are seen. Tics usually start in the eyes or face (blinking tics are most common) and then work their way down the body, to occur even in toes.

2

Signs and Symptoms

Typically, the onset of Tourette syndrome occurs around the age of six to seven years, and, as with other neurodevelopmental disorders, it occurs most commonly in boys. Tourette syndrome was previously thought to be rare, but recent community-based studies have indicated a prevalence of about 0.7 per cent in childhood (Scharf *et al.* 2012). The clinical history in Tourette syndrome is such that the tic symptoms will usually fluctuate in severity and frequency during the day as well as between the days, a phenomenon often referred to as 'waxing and waning'. This pattern may cause confusion as it may appear that the child only shows tics in certain situations, but the nature of the tics is such that the tics do indeed 'come and go'. A child with Tourette syndrome is likely to have many different motor and vocal tics, but head and neck tics are the most common, as many people with Tourette syndrome report, as demonstrated in Figure 2.1.

Coprolalia, the use of obscene or unacceptable language, rarely occurs in young children and occurs in only a minority of adults with Tourette syndrome, so this is certainly not diagnostic (Cavanna and Rickards 2013). Other unusual and rare symptoms include:

- copropraxia: obscene or unacceptable gestures

- coprographia: the urge to write obscene words

- echolalia: repeating other people's words

- echopraxia: repeating other people's gestures

- paliphenomena: repeating one's own words, phrases or sounds.

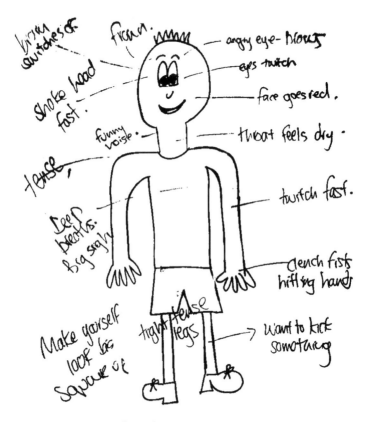

Figure 2.1 Motor and vocal tics

Other tics are common but rarely enquired about, such as toe tics, which can be upsetting or annoying to a child, even though few other people might be aware of their occurrence. As tics can occur in any muscle, some children report painful abdominal tics. Spitting is another rare and unusual tic which may be associated with a feeling of having excess saliva or may be related to a phobia and thus a *feeling of needing to spit out germs.*

Premonitory sensation

Many individuals with tics and Tourette syndrome describe a sensation or 'premonitory feeling' prior to a tic that is separate from the actual tic itself. The sensation is often an urge, impulse, tension, itch or tingling feeling that appears just before the tic (Kurlan, Lichter and Hewitt 1989). If the person is prevented from performing the tic, there is often a transitory increase in the sensory urge. Once the tic has been performed, there is a feeling of relief reported as the sensory urge being reduced. Sometimes young people report a need to reach a 'just right' feeling with the tics, which may be a response to the premonitory sensation.

Suggestibility

Many children and adolescents report an urge to perform a tic when they see others with tic disorders or hear a tic being described. For many individuals with tics, talking about tics is enough to prompt a bout of movements and/or sounds. Often in the clinic, when the clinician mentions a type of tic, the child has an urge to carry out that particular tic.

Control over the tics

Many children can suppress their tics for a brief period of time. This is often a conscious act that the child has learnt, particularly in certain places, such as school or when on stage. A degree of tension is involved in controlling the tics. We often tell families that it is a bit like blinking. You can stop blinking and keep your eyes open for several seconds, maybe a minute or even two, and cancel out a few blinks, but sooner or later, you have to blink. This is the same for tics: they can be controlled with practice but it can be hard work, especially at the beginning. Following much practice, a child can have a degree of control over the tics but this is only partial; this is described in much more detail in Chapter 5, which describes psychological treatments for tics. Often tic control takes place in school time or certain lessons. It is thus not surprising that when the child comes home from school, the tics can seem explosive. He[1] will have been controlling tics during the day, has likely run out of energy to continue to do so, and probably does not have the same reinforcers, such as teasing, commenting and uninvited attention from his classmates or teachers, to continue holding the tics in.

Stress and relaxation

Although stress does not cause tics, it can exacerbate tics. This may be in a certain lesson or before exams. When children are excited, the tics can also be more pronounced. Tics are often reported to be more intense around birthdays or special events. Paradoxically, when the child is relaxed, the tics may also be more apparent. As mentioned above, children often control the tics when at school and thus release the tics when at home as they are in a more relaxed environment. If children are 'ticcing' at home, then it is a good sign as they are probably feeling relaxed and comfortable to be themselves. Even though it is a natural thing to do, it is helpful not to comment on the variations that you might see in your child's tics.

---

1. Please note that we have used male pronouns throughout for ease of reading, except when referring to specific situations.

Many children with tics often report headaches. This may be related to the tension involved in controlling tics or directly related to the frequent movement of the head and neck. Some medicines used to treat associated symptoms can also bring on headaches and should therefore be discussed with your child's doctor.

Tics often increase in severity up to and during puberty, frequently reaching a relatively stable plateau during early adulthood. Interestingly, one particular longitudinal study (Pappert *et al.* 2003) showed that when a group of young adults who had experienced Tourette syndrome as children were contacted some years after having been treated, most of them indicated that they had grown out of the tics. However, when formally assessed, it appeared that the subjective ratings of tics were not accurate and many of the young adults continued to have some form of tics. Importantly, it is not that the individuals were denying that they had tics but more likely that they had become used to the tics and rarely acknowledged them. It is also probable that the level of impairment or impact on the adults' lives was far lower than it had been when they were known to the clinic as children.

Tics as part of a spectrum of neurodevelopmental disorders

In our clinics, we often see children with tics and related co-occurring symptoms. These are highlighted in detail in Part 3 of this book. The co-occurring symptoms may include obsessive compulsive behaviour, attention problems, dyspraxia or social skills deficits. Sometimes the symptoms may not fully meet the threshold for a diagnosis, but nevertheless, the child has the symptoms and may be impaired as a result. It is thus important that parents and teachers are aware of the co-occuring difficulties that may be present as well as the individual tics. We sometimes call this 'mixed neurodevelopmental symptoms'. Child and adolescent mental health clinics have many children who present in this way and it is easy for clinicians to miss the difficulties if they do not ask about them.

Assessment

The history of clinical symptoms should determine whether a child has transient tics, chronic tics or Tourette syndrome. The body part, severity and frequency of tics as well as precipitating and relieving factors should be recorded. Co-occurring symptoms such as those of attention deficit hyperactivity disorder (ADHD) and obsessive compulsive disorder (OCD) should also be discussed with the family, as is detailed in Part 3.

It is important to enquire how the child is affected by the tics in relation to daily functioning at home and at school, and also to ask about the child's self-esteem.

A family history of tics or OCD should be recorded. A good medication history is especially important since for a small number of children with ADHD, taking stimulant medication may have precipitated or exacerbated tics. It is helpful to understand the types of triggers that the child might have for his tics. Examples of common triggers might be playing on the computer, watching TV, feeling anxious in unfamiliar or quiet situations (such as at the cinema), feeling relaxed or during homework tasks. Similarly, understanding the contexts which appear to be associated with fewer tics can also be enlightening, such as when the child is focused on an activity, at school in the classroom or when he is playing a musical instrument. Figure 2.2 lists specific factors described by a group of children with Tourette syndrome.

School-related issues worth asking about include whether there is any bullying and teasing taking place and also the child's academic abilities.

The assessment is complete with a mental state examination and often a neurological examination of the child. A good history and neurological examination will distinguish tics from other movement disorders such as tardive dyskinesia or chorea, as described in Table 2.1.

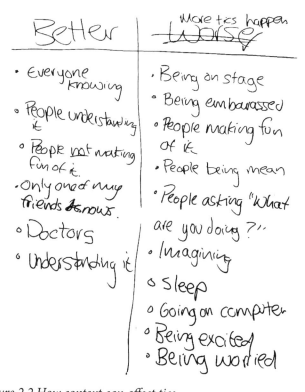

Figure 2.2 How context can affect tics

The key features of tics that distinguish them from other movement disorders are:

- They 'wax and wane'.

- There is variation in the anatomical site of tics.

- Tics may be temporarily suppressed.

- They are sometimes associated with a premonitory urge.

Table 2.1 Other movement disorders

Athetosis	Random involuntary movements occurring slowly, seeming to 'flow' to different parts of the body. Movements of upper limbs may resemble writing actions.
Ballismus	Rapid, large amplitude, almost 'flinging' movements.
Chorea	Involuntary, irregular, purposeless movements that 'flow' into one another randomly. Appears 'dance-like'. Affects distal muscles more than proximal.
Dystonia	Involuntary sustained muscle contractions that produce twisting or squeezing movements. May affect posture.
Myoclonus	Sudden brief muscle movements which may be due to muscle contraction or loss of muscle tone.
Tardive dyskinesia	Involuntary slow twisting movements related to side effects of long-term neuroleptic medication.
Tremor	Rhythmic oscillation around one or more focal points, usually a joint.

As children and adolescents may suppress their tics in the clinic, it is often a good idea to observe the young person for tics as he leaves the room and enter the corridor at the end of the interview. It can also be helpful to encourage a parent to bring in a diary (video or recorded on paper) of when and how often tics the occur, and particular frequent or difficult tics, although it is unhelpful to encourage parents to do this form of recording for an extended period of time as it can overly emphasise the family's focus on tics.

A number of assessment tools exist which help clarify the diagnosis but are also useful to monitor progress and in research. The most widely used and validated of these measures is the Yale Global Tic Severity Scale (YGTSS, Leckman *et al.* 1989), which has separate scales for motor and vocal tic severity and impairment. There are also briefer questionnaires such as the Parent Tic Questionnaire (Chang *et al.* 2009), which can be completed before an assessment by the parent and helpfully includes a brief list of motor and vocal tics.

Neuroradiological investigations such as electroence-phalogram (EEG) and structural magnetic resonance imaging (MRI) tend to look normal. If Wilson's disease, an autosomal recessive genetic disorder in which copper builds up in tissues, is suspected, then an assessment for serum copper is essential but, otherwise blood tests are not helpful in diagnosing Tourette syndrome. A more detailed description of helpful investigations for health professionals assessing individuals with Tourette syndrome is set out in the European guidelines on assessment of children and adults with Tourette syndrome (Cath *et al.* 2011).

Differential diagnosis

A good history is usually enough to establish the diagnosis of tic disorder from other disorders. Neuropsychiatric disorders associated with tics include autism, attention deficit hyperactivity disorder, obsessive compulsive disorder, schizophrenia and intellectual disability. Other disorders with a clear genetic basis, such as Huntington's chorea and Wilson's disease, or acquired motor tics such as those associated with trauma, encephalitis or Sydenham's chorea, should also be considered. Sometimes medicines can induce or worsen tics; these include stimulants, antipsychotics, antidepressants and some antiepileptics such as carbamezipine.

3

Causes of Tic Disorders

Although the precise cause is unknown, several studies support the fact that Tourette syndrome is an inherited, developmental disorder affecting nerve transmission. This results in changes in a complex pathway of the brain known as the the 'cortico-striatal-thalamic-cortical circuit' (Felling and Singer 2011). People with Tourette syndrome probably have a genetic vulnerability to developing tics, with associated structural and/or functional changes in the brain circuitry.

Genetics

We often see that several people from the same family will experience tics. It may be the case that the presence of tics in family members skips one or two generations, but more than half of children seen in clinic will have parents who can identify a family member with tics or other commonly experienced conditions such as obsessive compulsive disorder.

Evidence that Tourette syndrome is a genetic disorder comes from twin studies looking at concordance rates (i.e. cases where both twins have the same symptoms). The twin studies show that monozygotic twins (same egg and thus identical) have an 86 per cent concordance rate for chronic tic disorder compared with 20 per cent concordance in dizygotic (non-identical) twins (Hyde *et al.* 1992; Price *et al.* 1985). This suggests that genes do play a part in the causes of Tourette syndrome.

In studies where both twins are affected, usually one twin's symptoms may be more severe than the other, suggesting that although Tourette syndrome is inherited, there is a great deal of variability in the expression of the condition. This may be due to environmental factors before or at birth or even later in childhood.

Genetics is a complicated subject, but it is basically the study of chromosomes. Chromosomes make us what we are – they carry all the information to help the cell to survive and develop. In other words, they contain our genetic information. Our cells each have 23 matching pair of chromosomes. Chromosomes are made from long coiled molecules of deoxyribonucleic acid (DNA). A shorter region of DNA that carries the genetic code for a particular characteristic or cell activity is called a gene, as shown in Figure 3.1.

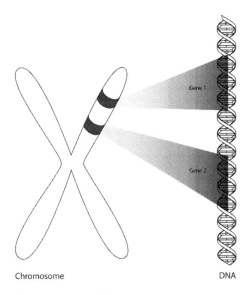

Chromosome   DNA

Figure 3.1 Chromosomes and genes

In Tourette syndrome, the particular characteristic or cell activity that is of interest may be related to a gene that affects the production of chemicals or neurotransmitters that are involved in inhibiting movement, controlling impulses, development of obsessions and so on.

When scientists study genetics, they use a number of techniques such as genetic linkage, or looking at the molecular structure and function of the genes. Genetic linkage is the tendency of genes that are close together on a chromosome to be inherited together. Linkage studies investigating Tourette syndrome thus involve looking closely at a marker gene on a chromosome and identifying patterns of inheritance amongst people with Tourette syndrome. Several studies have suggested the importance of certain chromosomal regions, including 4, 5, 11 and 17 (Tourette Syndrome Association International Consortium for Genetics 1999). Other studies have highlighted markers on chromosomes 2, 6, 8, 11, 14, 20 and 21 (Simonic *et al.* 2001).

Other genetic studies involve looking at the structure of the chromosome to see if there are any defects or deviations on the chromosome itself. Several cytogenetic abnormalities have been reported in patients with Tourette syndrome, including abnormalities on chromosomes 2, 7, 6, 8 and 18 (Crawford *et al.* 2003; Kroisel *et al.* 2001; Verkerk *et al.* 2003).

Various candidate genes have been assessed, including those for dopamine receptors, dopamine transporters, noradrenergic genes and a few serotonergic genes. It is most likely that there is no one single gene that is involved in causing Tourette syndrome but that several genes contribute to the likelihood that a child will develop chronic tics. This is especially likely given that Tourette syndrome so commonly co-occurs with other neurodevelopmental conditions, which also likely have several chromosomes involved in their expression.

In summary, although the genetic studies are complex, we can say that children with tics are often seen in families where there are several members with tics or a history of OCD. We can also say that if your twin has tics, you are more likely to develop tics if you are an identical twin than if you are a non-identical twin.

Despite the advancement of technology, no definitive causative gene has yet been found to be linked with the development of Tourette syndrome.

The brain

Tourette syndrome is a complex condition involving tics that occur episodically in bouts in many different parts of the body, often with premonitory sensory urges, suggestibility, associated OCD or ADHD and occasionally the use of emotion-laden words such as swearing. So what part of the brain would account for all the above symptoms in Tourette syndrome? It is fair to say that several brain regions and their connections are affected rather than one specific area. Due to the variability of the severity and range of symptoms, and the way behaviour and brain activity and structure are measured, it is hard to make sense of research studies. The most important structures in the brain and spinal cord associated with tics are outlined in Figure 3.2.

The two main areas involved in TS are the cortex and the striatum. Brain studies have shown evidence that the cortico-striatal-thalamic-cortical pathways are involved in expression of tics (Felling and Singer 2011). This is a circuit connecting the cortex to the striatum and thalamus and back again to the cortex. What exactly is the role of these brain regions?

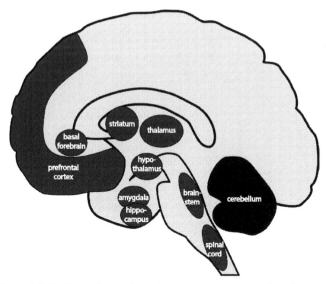

Figure 3.2 Brain and spinal cord structures associated with tics

Cortex

The cortex is the outer bit of the brain, the so-called 'grey matter'. The prefrontal part of the cortex is right at the front of the cortex. The prefrontal cortex is involved in planning, organisation and attentional skills. It is also important for concentration, emotions, impulses, obsessions, compulsions and movement.

Striatum

The striatum is a component of the basal ganglia, which contain a group of cells (nuclei) that are involved in facilitating voluntary movement. The basal ganglia receive information about a type of movement from the cortex. The basal ganglia will then help by selecting the appropriate action by initiating movement and inhibiting opposing movement. The basal ganglia include the caudate nucleus and the nucleus accumbens. The caudate is involved in movement but also many other functions.

Thalamus

The thalamus is often described as a 'relay station' since most sensory information (except smell) first passes in the thalamus before being sent on to other areas of the brain. The thalamus is divided into a number of nuclei that are specialised to deal with different types of sensory information.

Limbic system

The limbic system is a set of nerves and networks that are involved in mood, emotions and drives. It includes the hippocampus, hypothalamus, amygdala and anterior thalamus.

Amygdala

The amygdala is housed within the limbic system. It is the emotion centre of the brain and involved in fear, anxiety and panic.

Children with Tourette syndrome have been shown to have larger prefrontal cortical regions than their peers without the condition. Functional imaging studies have shown that tic suppression involves activation and alteration of the prefrontal cortex (Peterson *et al.* 1998; Peterson *et al.* 2001), and reduced white matter in the corpus callosum, the band of nerve fibres joining the two brain hemispheres (Plessen *et al.* 2006). Other studies have demonstrated that impaired inhibition at the motor cortex leads to tics. Various neuroimaging studies have shown reduced caudate volume and reduced activity in the caudate. Research has also described a subgroup of children with Tourette syndrome who do not have ADHD but appear to have strong connections in white matter (which connects up the brain) and show relative strengths with inhibiting and directing their behaviour (Jackson *et al.* 2007, 2015), which the authors suggest may result from a frequent habit of controlling tics.

Neurotransmitters

Within the various parts of the brain, all actions, feelings and thoughts are generated at a chemical level. It is the neurotransmitters that are responsible for the brain carrying out its functions, whether that is movement, inhibition, thinking or planning. Neurotransmitters are chemical messengers that transmit signals across nerve endings. There are several neurotransmitters in the brain, all having different functions. The main neurotransmitters involved in expression of tics include dopamine, serotonin and gamma-aminobutyric acid (GABA).

You can see in Figures 6.1 and 6.2 (in Chapter 6 on medication) that the brain regions involved in Tourette syndrome (i.e. the prefrontal cortex and striatum) are saturated with receptors for the neurotransmitters dopamine and serotonin. It is thus not surprising that many of the medicines used in Tourette syndrome have an effect on these neurotransmitters.

Dopamine

Dopamine is a neurotransmitter involved in regulating movement, reward, pleasure and cognition. It is also involved in psychosis. Tics can be suppressed by medication such as dopamine antagonists (dopamine blocking) and exacerbated by dopamine agonists. The dopamine antagonists are often used to treat psychosis-type illness such as schizophrenia. Several neuroimaging studies show that people with TS have higher densities of presynaptic dopamine transporters and postsynaptic dopamine D2 receptors in the basal ganglia. This is also found in postmortem studies of people with TS. However, the cortico-striatal-thalamic-cortical circuit contains several other neurotransmitters besides dopamine systems, including serotoninergic, glutamatergic, GABAergic, noradrenergic and opioid systems. This suggests that various neurotransmitters are involved in generating tics, explaining why no one single drug is effective.

Serotonin

Serotonin is a neurotransmitter involved in mood, anxiety, obsessive symptoms and sleep.

Gamma-aminobutyric acid

Gamma-aminobutyric acid (GABA) functions as an inhibitory neurotransmitter meaning it blocks neurotransmision. An increase in GABA may allow more control over tics.

Environment

Pregnancy

There have been studies demonstrating that a subset of children with Tourette syndrome had birth difficulties, including induced labour, cord around the neck, forceps delivery, neonatal jaundice, caesarean section and prolonged labour. The most consistent reported risk factors for Tourette syndrome are maternal smoking, nausea and vomiting during first trimester and low birth weight (Leckman 2002).

Male sex is recognised as a risk factor, leading to the hypothesis that androgen (the male hormone) exposure during critical periods in fetal brain development increases development of tics (Peterson et al. 1992). Some researchers conclude that onset of Tourette syndrome may be associated with changes in the dopaminergic system as a result of early brain injury. However, it is most likely that a baby is born with a genetic sensitivity to having Tourette syndrome, which is expressed if he experiences a particular event, or perhaps several events.

PANDAS

Paediatric autoimmune neuropsychiatric disorders associated with streptococcal infections, often referred to as PANDAS, was first recognised in 1998 (Swedo *et al*. 1998) and relates to a subset of children who present suddenly with OCD and/or tics. The condition is said to be caused by a streptococcal throat infection.

Diagnostic criteria include:

- acute onset of OCD and/or tics

- onset occurs before puberty

- onset is dramatic

- symptoms decrease significantly between episodes

- association with streptococcal infection, i.e. positive throat culture or rising anti-streptococcal antibody titres

- associated neuropsychiatric abnormalities such as anxiety, restlessness, hypersensitivity, irritability, developmental regression including 'baby talk' and deterioration in handwriting.

Neuroimaging studies have shown that some individuals with this constellation of symptoms have large basal ganglia, indicating possible brain inflammation (Giedd *et al*. 2000).

It is thought that the streptococcal bacteria have molecules on their cell walls that are similar to molecules in the human body in areas such as the heart, joints and brain tissue. The body, however, recognises the molecules as foreign and then the immune system produces antibodies to these molecules. Unfortunately, the antibodies then react with the human host molecules, such as in the heart and brain.

The diagnosis of PANDAS is a clinical one based on history. Laboratory tests can be useful, such as throat cultures that show group A beta-haemolytic streptococcal bacteria (Dale and Heyman 2002). Strep infections will also trigger the onset of anti-streptococcal antibodies which are measured by titres. Titres will be low at the beginning of symptoms and should increase over the next few weeks as the body produces more antibodies.

Table 3.1 PANDAS, PANS and CANS

PANDAS	PANS	CANS
Sudden onset of OCD and/or tic disorder	Sudden onset of OCD or severe restricted food intake	Sudden onset of OCD
Association with streptococcal infection	Two of the following: anxiety, emotional lability, irritability, developmental regression, deterioration in school performance, somatic signs such as sleep problems, enuresis or increased urinary frequency	Other features such as: anxiety, psychosis, developmental regression, sensitivity to sensory stimuli, emotional lability tics, dysgraphia, clumsiness, hyperactivity
Motor hyperactivity and neurological movements		

The above condition is controversial mainly because of the diagnostic criteria and the difficulty of demonstrating a direct link to streptococcal infection. Many children have streptococcal throat infections but they do not have PANDAS symptoms. Some children have acute-onset OCD but no streptococcal infection. This led to researchers developing new criteria for a condition called paediatric acute-onset neuropsychiatric syndrome (PANS), which recognises acute-onset OCD but also severely restricted food intake and additional neuropsychiatric symptoms (Swedo, Leckman and Rose 2012). Other researchers have identified a similar condition known as idiopathic childhood acute neuropsychiatric syndromes (CANS), where the onset of symptoms could be due to infection, drugs, toxins, vascular irregularity, hypoxic or autoimmune conditions (Singer *et al.* 2012).

Despite all the controversy, it is recognised that there is a subgroup of children who present with sudden-onset acute OCD with or without tics. That is the main difference with this cohort of conditions and 'regular' Tourette syndrome; the symptoms come on suddenly and are abrupt, often described as dramatic in onset.

Thus in summary, a specific cause for tics or Tourette syndrome has not yet been identified, but since the expression of Tourette syndrome is so variable, several aetiological factors have been identified, involving genetics and the environment.

Part 2

Management

4

Working with Schools

A good understanding by teachers and other school staff of children's neurodevelopmental challenges leads to the most positive experience of school and the most resilient children. This rule certainly applies to children with Tourette syndrome, as tics are often very visible to other people. A positive experience at school can not only equip the child well in managing the tics but also help him to know that challenges in life are surmountable with understanding and correct support.

Tics can interfere with attention, and be disruptive and overwhelming – a description referred to as 'neurological chaos' by Leslie Packer and Sherry Pruitt in their excellent book *Challenging Kids, Challenged Teachers: Teaching Students with Tourette's, Bipolar Disorder, Executive Dysfunction, OCD, ADHD, and More* (2010). It is important that teachers also understand about any co-occurring conditions that the child may have and ensure that the relevant information is shared about the difficulties. Tics can interfere with schoolwork in a physical way, such as hand movements being disruptive during writing tasks and eye movements interfering with reading. The constant ticcing can also affect concentration and make it difficult to think for an extended period of time. Tics can be uncomfortable or painful for some children as well as being embarrassing (such as use of socially inappropriate words or gestures). These elements can make it difficult to remain in the classroom for extended periods but it is important that the child tries to do so (with whatever adaptations are needed) to ensure that he can access the curriculum and are included with his peers. Figure 4.1 shows how a ten-year-old boy with Tourette syndrome describes how the condition affects his experience of school.

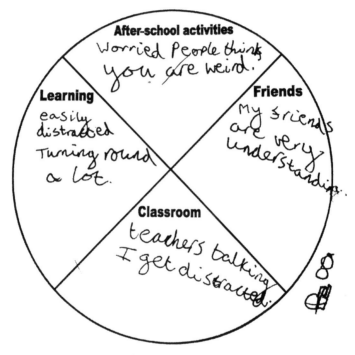

Figure 4.1 TS and school

It is important that a child with Tourette syndrome is placed in a supportive environment where the staff understand or are willing to develop an understanding of Tourette syndrome and the child's particular needs. Unfortunately, tics are usually at their most frequent during the pre-teen years when children are transitioning between junior and senior school, and therefore this is a time to be particularly vigilant that all of your child's teachers are fully prepared with sensible and accurate information. It is very helpful to contact your child's secondary school before he starts the first year. Booking an individual appointment in which to describe your child's needs, emphasising his strengths and weaknesses, and providing helpful, accurate information can be hugely helpful.

It is important to plan ahead and to ensure that before the end of the school year contact is made with a new teacher to facilitate an understanding about what tics are and are not, the pattern of how they change with time, what factors exacerbate the tics at school and effective coping strategies that have been used to date.

As tics are visible to everyone, it is important to target not merely the class teacher with information but all of the staff at school, including support teachers and non-academic staff.

The following key points are important to share with school staff:

- Tics fluctuate and change over time – some days children may have many tics of many types and other days very few.

- Tics are suggestible in that if a child has a cold and starts to sniff, the sniffing can continue for long after the illness has gone.

- Tics can look like mimicry. Sometimes, children with tics can pick up gestures, words or intonation from another person (including a teacher) which they cannot control and may not even be aware of.

- Although a child might be able to control some tics some of the time, he will not be successful all the time.

- Not all children respond to behavioural or medication therapy.

- Tics are not the fault of the child or the child's parents.

- Having tics can make a child tired.

- Having tics is not a good reason to feel sorry for or excuse the child from certain activities.

- Suppressing tics may distract the child from tasks at times, but if the child appears to have difficulties with learning this is unlikely to be only due to the tics and other reasons for the learning difficulties should be explored with the child's teachers.

Recent studies (Nussey, Pistrang and Murphy 2014) have shown that giving teachers talks and leaflets about a particular condition or conditions can improve a child's educational experience considerably. Sometimes parents worry about doing this for fear of 'labelling the child'. However, with sensible information, teachers cope well and can facilitate an understanding in the classmates of the child.

Giving a presentation to the classmates of a child with Tourette syndrome can be very beneficial. We carried out a study a few years ago (Nussey, Pistrang and Murphy 2013) in which four children and their teachers gave a brief presentation on Tourette syndrome to their class. The information was developed by our clinical team and colleagues at Tourettes Action in the UK. The results from the study showed that the children benefited from the presentation. Children reported a better understanding of the condition and showed more tolerance of the child with tics, and the teachers reported feeling more confident in being able to deal with the needs of the child with tics. Importantly, the parents of the children also felt more confident that their child could cope in school. Interestingly, children with tics who chose to remain in the classroom during the presentation by their teacher, as opposed to those who left the room, seemed to benefit most from the brief but helpful intervention.

Building resiliency and an ability for the child to know that it is sensible to explain to other people about their tics is key in living with Tourette syndrome, and nothing reinforces this message more than a parent and teacher who support a child in informing the child's peers with well-thought-out and accurate information.

In addition to ensuring that everyone understands about Tourette syndrome, there are other ways to support a child with Tourette syndrome in the classroom:

- Having the student seated at the side of the classroom: not the front where tics are visible, but not at the back where he may be easily distracted.

- Seating the child beside easygoing and tolerant peers, which can reduce negative responses to difficult tics.

- Not allowing the child to avoid certain activities such as reading or writing because of his tics. It is much better to accommodate the child in completing the task even if it requires more work and thought from his teacher.

- Regular support between home and school. Regular, brief communication via email can be best and is discreet. It is important to remember to communicate about areas that are going well and not only about problems that need solving.

- Having a space to 'tic in peace', which can be useful if a student feels overwhelmed. Stress and anxiety can exacerbate tics so if a child feels in control it may even reduce the level of tics overall. However, it is important that these 'tic breaks' are not as and when a child requests them but are regulated. Giving the child with tics a regular job such as delivering messages to other rooms or giving out the copy-books in the classroom can be very helpful. For older students it may be helpful to have more formal or organised breaks with a specific area to go to.

- Having a designated person or mentor for the child to approach when needed: this can be very beneficial and could ideally be set up at the beginning of each academic year.

- For students who tend to forget rules or get carried away in situations, giving them a contract which is reviewed regularly and supported by a reward system. This can be extremely helpful even if only needed for a limited period.

- Asking your child's specialist (this could be a medical doctor, occupational therapist, nurse or psychologist) to contact the school to suggest ways to support your child and provide staff with information about your child's specific symptoms of TS.

Bullying

The thought of their child with Tourette syndrome being teased and bullied often preys on a parent's mind. This is particularly the case when plans are made for the child to move from primary to secondary education. Reassuringly, children with Tourette syndrome are typically not bullied, so you should certainly not assume that this will happen. However, it is helpful to put plans in place to minimise the likelihood that it may occur and to act quickly should the child with TS report that another student has been unkind towards him. The most important prevention is to ensure that your child has a good capacity to live with his tics by using a clear and well-informed toolkit of strategies.

In his toolkit, the child should have a good understanding of the basics of tics and Tourette syndrome, as described in Part 1 of this book. There are also several helpful books listed in the Useful Resources and Websites section of this book, which you can share with your child. The child should be able to answer any question presented to him by a peer. He should be encouraged to ignore bullying and have a clear plan for what to do if he is teased or bullied (e.g. the child should speak with a parent/teacher as soon as possible). The child should understand that it is not his fault that another student is being unkind to him. Each school should have a bullying policy which they should follow immediately. Most commonly, if the bully is spoken to about the behaviour and the consequences of bullying, it should not re-occur. The child should be reassured that the bullying is not his fault.

A clear and open communication channel between parent and child is essential. Parents should remain calm and understand the whole situation as quickly as possible, although this is not always easy.

Communication is key

It helps a great deal if parents and teachers communicate well. Most children with Tourette syndrome should have a supportive plan for their learning, behaviour and social and emotional functioning, with targets and strategies to achieve those targets (often referred to as an individual education plan). Meetings between parents and teachers should be organised to discuss and review targets. The structured demands of homework after school (particularly when the child or parent is tired) can also pose particular demands on both the child and his parents; if homework is causing stress at home this should be carefully discussed with the child's teachers or advisers at school. An emphasis on organisation and reasonable demands should be agreed between student, parents and teachers.

Research has shown that teachers tend to report fewer behavioural problems and attention difficulties than parents of children with TS (Christie and Jassi 2002). This may be because children with TS put a high level of effort into keeping it all together at school during the day (including controlling their tics) and then have lower resources when they arrive home after school. It is helpful to bear this potential pattern of behaviour in mind in discussions between teachers and parents. Different views regarding work can cause tension between parents and teachers, which will most likely be best managed through clear, regular communication and a good understanding of the child's personal strengths and weaknesses.

5

Psychological Management

Many children live easily with their tics while others can feel frustrated or embarrassed, or experience physical discomfort or pain from the movements and sounds. Research since the 1970s has seen the emergence and validation of several effective psychological treatments for children with tics.

Regardless of the form of treatment, an essential part of the intervention is that the child and everyone in his system (e.g. family, teachers and friends) understand Tourette syndrome. This understanding is the keystone to living with Tourette syndrome. Once the individual with tics understands about the condition this can enable him to cope with the day-to-day challenges that come as a result of having Tourette syndrome.

Psychological interventions tend to be behavioural, which means that they consist of the child learning activities or things he can do to change certain behaviours. Cognitive therapies have also been shown to be helpful, particularly for teenagers, who benefit from changing the way they think about their tics in addition to taking certain actions.

The most important reason for pursuing psychological treatment for your child is that he is bothered by the tics and ready to try treatment, not that you would like him to stop ticcing or that the symptoms bother his teachers or friends. It should always be remembered that psychological treatments are not a cure but may be an important part of the child's toolkit for living with tics.

Habit reversal training

The best scientifically supported behavioural treatment is called habit reversal training (HRT). This approach has been used since the 1970s. The most convincing studies showing HRT to be effective have been published since the early 2000s. Based on these studies, about two-thirds of children who received a package of behavioural therapy which included habit reversal training reduced their tics by about a third. Habit reversal training has been researched as a major component of a programme called comprehensive behavioural intervention for tics (CBITS). CBITs is a multi-component package, which includes habit reversal training, relaxation, functional analysis and social support. This programme draws on all of the elements of previous research which were thought to be effective in helping people to manage their tics.

The authors of CBITS (Woods, Conelea and Himle 2010) identify that for each individual, external and internal factors in his life maintain the tics.

An example of an external factor might be the experience of having another person comment on his tic in a critical way or a parent who gives the child a cuddle when he has been through a difficult day of tics. These actions inadvertently reward the tics and can serve to maintain tics, particularly in these situations. Once people in the child's environment are aware of this cycle then they can change it and the association will stop and the tics will reduce. This analysis of the causes and consequences of behaviour is referred to as 'functional analysis'.

An internal factor might be the tension that a child feels before he has a tic (a 'premonitory urge'). Children may have different words to describe the urge, such as tension, pressure, tickle or itch. In the treatment, the child becomes more aware of the urge (and the onset of a tic), which allows him to implement a behaviour before the tics occur to stop the tic. Figure 5.1 shows the association between the urge which precedes the tic, the tic occurring and the relief that occurs after the tic has been expressed. This pattern builds up a reinforcement cycle, in which the child continually expresses the tic in order to feel the relief of the urge.

Figure 5.1 Association between urge, tic and relief

In treatment, the therapist makes a list (called a hierarchy) of the current tics with the child. The therapist then guides the child in rating how annoying each of the tics in the hierarchy is for the child. The most annoying tic is selected from the list. The therapist discusses with the child exactly what happens when the tic is performed (e.g. an urge in the eyelid, followed by a wink and then a head jerk), referred to as a tic description. From there the child can increase his awareness of the urge to tic and when the tic itself is about to occur. This stage is called tic awareness. Once the child has a good awareness of the tic pattern, an exercise, referred to as a competing response (or a 'tic blocker' as described by Dr Duncan McKinlay; McKinlay 2015), is then identified. This is called 'devising a competing response'. The idea is that before a tic is performed, a competing response is used to control the tic. The child must be able to tolerate not giving in to the urge to tic and to hold the competing response until the feeling goes away.

Table 5.1 shows some commonly used competing responses.

Table 5.1 Competing responses

Motor tics	Competing response
Eye blinking	Controlled eye blinks
Arm jerks	Placing hand against leg
Lip licking	Placing tongue on roof of mouth
Vocal tics	
Sniffing	Slow breaths out through the nose and in through the mouth
Shouting words	Pursing lips

There is no 'perfect' competing response for any tic – the best strategy should be devised between the child and his therapist. It is helpful for the therapist to practise both the tic and the competing response himself to see what works and effectively controls the tic, and use it in sessions with the child for a period of time so that everyone is confident that the specific competing response works well.

Figure 5.2 shows the pattern in which a competing response is used to block a tic occurring. When the child is using a competing response he will not feel the relief and reduction in urge that occurs when he expresses the tic. Some parents may be concerned that this response will be uncomfortable for the child but this is not typically the case; quite quickly the child learns to tolerate the urge (and lack of relief) and is very pleased that he can control the tic successfully.

Figure 5.2 Using a competing response to block a tic

Some children find it relatively easy to use the competing response and with practice in everyday life it can occur quite automatically. Having said that, these children may be more able to control some of their tics generally, whereas for others it is much more difficult. Eye tics in particular can be difficult to control.

It is key to ensure that an effective competing response is selected from the beginning which is comfortable for the child. There are four rules which typically guide the selection of the competing response:

1. The tic cannot occur when a competing response is in place.

2. The competing response should be less socially noticeable than the tic itself.

3. It should be possible for the child to hold the competing response for at least a minute or until the urge goes away.

4. No props (e.g. trouser pockets) should be used in carrying out the competing response as these 'tools' may not always be available when needed.

Children learn the rules for selecting a competing response in treatment so that once treatment is complete they can then apply the technique to new tics which might occur in the future. It is important that the child tries the competing response while he is with the therapist to make sure that it is effective for the child and does not obstruct him carrying out typical daily activities such as reading, talking or playing games.

In fact, the most important point of therapy is that the child then starts to apply use of the competing response in his day-to-day activities when he thinks it is helpful. The choices he makes about when and how to control his tics might not always be what his family would predict and it is important for parents to be sensitive that it is up to the child where and when he uses the competing response. It can be helpful for the parents or teacher to praise the child when they see him using his tic-controlling exercise but they should not get into a nagging situation or comment when he is ticcing.

Exposure with response prevention

A second, fairly similar approach is called exposure with response prevention (ERP). In this approach, children first gain control over their tics by practising suppressing their tics for a period of time. In this approach, children don't have to figure out any actions to prevent their tics but instead try to 'hold them in' for as long as possible and increase the length of time that they can go without ticcing. In doing this they get used to the uncomfortable sensation which preceeds the tic and discover that it goes away with time even if they don't tic: a process referred to as habituation. In treatment, the focus on the urge which precedes is increased through talking about it and arranging activities in which the urge is very strong. The child and his family practice the exposure and response prevention most days during treatment and the child usually manages to control the tics for longer periods, even when the urge is strong.

This approach seems to be particularly helpful for younger children, or a child who has many tics he wants to control better. Again, children control their tics in situations that they choose, until it becomes easier. Many children, and indeed adults, with tic report spontaneous and regular use of a tic suppression strategy even without formal treatment to learn it (Matsuda *et al.* 2016), and interestingly, individuals who report being able to control their tics effectively also appear to report a higher quality of life generally.

Both of these types of therapy have now been shown to be effective for children as young as five years old, although naturally, support from parents and teachers is likely to be even more important for younger than older children.

Given that tics wax and wane and change with time, the advantage of learning a successful strategy to manage tics is that should another annoying tic present itself, then the child will hopefully have developed the tools for dealing with it.

Over time, carrying out 'tic control' tends to become more automatic for the individual with tics. It can be compared to the enormous effort required when a person first learns any procedural activity, such as how to ride a bicycle, touch-type or knit. With practice, the task becomes more automatic, easier and more efficient. The child finds that he is able to carry out the task while he engages in everyday behaviours such as a talking, writing, eating or playing a computer game.

Social support

The parent is often a co-therapist in treatment in that they offer encouragement and support for when the child is using his competing response and continue to ignore the involuntary tics when they occur. Giving praise, which often results in your child feeling good about using the strategies, will probably help him to learn all the more effectively too.

Many therapists use a reward system with the child and family to maintain motivation, particularly on the difficult days when other important events distract the child from focusing on controlling his tics. It is also important to remember that commenting on the tics themselves is not helpful but that noticing when the child has successfully managed to control a tic with a smile or a nod can be very encouraging. You can then reward your child for actively working on his tics but ignore a tic when it happens to come through, which may be because your child was focused on something more important than controlling his tics.

Unfortunately, research from both the UK and the US shows that there is limited awareness and too few therapists trained in delivering behavioural therapy to people with Tourette syndrome (Woods *et al.* 2010). Sometimes doctors are not aware of the research supporting behavioural and psychological treatments for tics, and families may not know to bring it up with the clinician caring for their child. If your child is bothered by his tics or they cause them discomfort, you could use the information in this chapter to inform your child's clinician about this form of therapy and enquire about any provision of treatment locally or at a specialist clinic.

Innovations

Recently, there have been several innovations that increase the availability of behavioural treatments. The first exciting adaptation is that of CBITS being offered using telemedicine (e.g. Skype), in which the therapist and the child can work together while not sitting in the same room. Studies and our own clinical experience show that this is an acceptable way to deliver treatment and works just as well as sitting face to face in the same room (Himle *et al.* 2012; Ricketts *et al.* 2015b). This means that families can live several hundred miles away from their therapist but still receive effective treatment.

Another approach is called intensive outpatient treatment (Blount *et al.* 2014), in which the child receives CBITs or ERP intensively during two to three consecutive days with a follow-up appointment several weeks after, giving the child and family time to practise the strategies to integrate them into the child's everyday life. Again, we have experience of this working very well for families in which it is not practical to travel to a specialist clinic each week for an extended period of time.

Given the benefits that people with Tourette syndrome and their family can have from meeting other people with Tourette syndrome, we have adapted the CBITS programme to be delivered within a group of children (typically 6–11 children) and their families all at the same time. Tic reduction immediately after treatment is slightly less than in individual treatment. Follow-up reports one year after the group treatment showed that the children continued to have fewer tics than children in a comparison group. Importantly, school attendance appeared to be higher after the CBITS group, and tic control was also strong, which appeared to be associated with a more positive quality of life (Yates *et al.* 2016). It has been found that the group approach reduces waiting lists for treatment, makes optimal use of therapists and also trains up junior staff and colleagues from community clinics to be competent at delivering the treatment. However, in order to have enough children to attend a group a service will need to have a sufficient number of referrals of children with Tourette syndrome who are bothered by their tics.

More recently, researchers in Europe and North America have adapted educational material and made behavioural therapy programmes available on a website (e.g. www.tichelper.com). Some programmes only involve accessing the intervention through the website with no interaction with a therapist, whereas in others, the child works with a therapist mainly using emails and texts as they follow the programme on a computer. We are still waiting to see how successful these approaches are and how acceptable families find them, but they certainly are promising in terms of offering treatment to more people, especially those who do not live close to specialist centres.

Positively, recent studies have shown that it does not have to be a psychologist who offers treatment. Effective treatment from clinics with occupational therapists (Rowe, Yuen and Dure 2013) and nurses (Ricketts *et al.* 2015a) who have had appropriate training and receive the relevant supervision can also deliver helpful intervention.

Myths

There are common myths about behavioural therapies for tics which have been thought to make parents uncertain about seeking help for their child with tics. It's helpful to know the tics and the work that has been done to test out the myths:

If my child holds his tics in won't they all just burst out later when he stops?

Studies show that practising holding tics in reduces tics overall. And even if we measure tics just after a child has been holding them in for a while we don't see a 'rebound'; if anything, they go down slightly.

If my child stops one tic won't his other tics just get worse?

The opposite is actually true: when looked at in studies, it has been discovered that learning to control some tics might actually make all your tics slightly better – even the tics you haven't worked on.

If my child is busy fighting his tics won't he find it difficult to pay attention to anything else?

When children first learn to control their tics it definitely takes some effort, so perhaps practising in a key lesson or exam might not be the best idea. However, the effect on their attention is small and probably fades as the child get better at it.

If my child meets other children with tics will he catch new tics off them?

It is true that tics are suggestible and children may briefly catch new tics from others with tics. These tic bouts are short-lived, however (they usually last only a day or two).

Living with Tourette syndrome

Recently, research has turned towards evaluating more broadly focused psychological treatments which attempt to equip children with the tools to live with Tourette syndrome rather than just to control their tics, although naturally, this may also be an important part of the adaptation. An intervention designed to take a wider focus to include tics, self-esteem, anxiety management, management of attention and hyperactivity challenges has been highlighted as being effective (McGuire *et al.* 2015).

6

Medication

It is important to know from the outset that to date, there is no specific drug that can bring about total permanent cessation of tics. All that medication can do at best is to reduce the frequency or intensity of tics for a period of time. Therefore, it should be stressed that the aim of using medication is to allow the child to function at school and home at an acceptable level.

The lowest possible therapeutic dosage of medication should be used, and the dose adjusted to achieve therapeutic effects, watching out for possible side effects. Parents and children should be reminded of the nature of tics, (i.e. that the condition will wax and wane, and that it may be necessary to increase the drug during waxing of tics). The clinician and family should monitor the outcome, whether it is tic reduction in terms of frequency or severity, or improvement in psychological well-being. Rating scales, as mentioned in Part 1, can often be useful to help monitor tic frequency.

Most experts agree that different medicines should be tried at different times during the course and development of a child's tic disorder. We have found that sometimes restarting a drug that was tried previously and had not been helpful may even be effective the second time around. There is thus a trial-and-error approach to using medication but unfortunately the choice of medicines is limited.

Indications

There are numerous guidelines and papers reviewing the use of medication. For more detailed information on dosage and side effects, please see Roessner *et al.* 2011. Generally, medication should be considered in the following circumstances:

- Pain or discomfort: the sudden repetitive nature of tics can be very painful, particularly head and neck tics. Occasionally tics can cause headaches or migraines.

- Self-harm: some tics involve repetitively hitting oneself or other forms of self-harm.

- Social problems: unfortunately it is often other people's reactions to tics that can cause the most stress. Sometimes tics are so severe that the child or young person will want to withdraw from social groups. The anxiety this creates should not be underestimated.

- Functional impairment: tics may prevent a child working in school either via the nature of the tic, such as with handwriting or performing a task, or because the physical and mental exhaustion of holding on to tics in the classroom can be overwhelming.

Scientific basis of medication

As mentioned in Part 1, there is evidence of dysfunction in neurotransmitter pathways in the brains of people with Tourette syndrome. Studies support the hypothesis of an imbalance in the dopaminergic system. This is not surprising given the abundance of dopamine receptors in the key areas of the brain in Tourette syndrome, as shown in Figure 6.1. Studies have shown increased numbers of striatal and cortical dopamine receptors and differences in binding to dopamine transporters in the basal ganglia and release of dopamine following use of stimulants. Thus, modulating the dopaminergic metabolism by blocking the postsynaptic D2 receptors is the main action of medication used in management of Tourette syndrome.

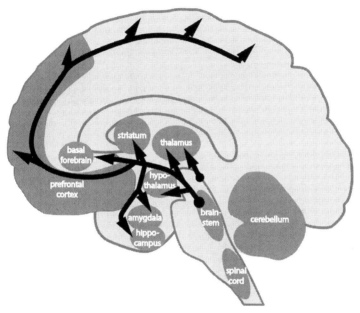

Figure 6.1 Dopamine pathways

Dopaminergic systems dominate in Tourette syndrome, but other systems such as serotoninergic, noradrenergic, glutamatergic, GABAergic and opioid systems all play a part. The serotonin pathways are shown in Figure 6.2.

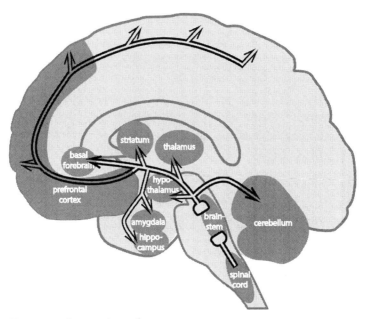

Figure 6.2 Serotonin pathways

It is likely that all these systems interconnect and all have some role.

Neuroleptic medication

The neuroleptic medicines are a group of drugs that block dopamine receptors in the basal ganglia in the brain. In particular they block the D2 dopamine receptor. This leads to a reduction in tics but, unfortunately, high blockage of the receptors can also lead to side effects.

Haloperidol and pimozide have been used since the 1960s and found to be effective in randomised double-blind controlled trials (Sallee *et al.* 1997; Shapiro *et al.* 1989). These are studies where the child does not know what he or she has taken and the person rating the outcomes does not know either. The allocation of drug to each child is random to avoid any bias. Pimozide is rarely used in the UK in children due to cardiac effects picked up on electrocardiogram (ECG) monitoring.

Side effects for both pimozide and haloperidol include other movement problems such as dystonia and restlessness (akathisia), and pseudo-Parkinson's as a result of the dopamine blockage. Other side effects include onset of anxiety, hyperprolactinaemia and increased appetite leading to weight gain.

Benzamides

The benzamides such as sulpiride and amisulpiride are also selective D2 dopamine receptor antagonists. As they are highly selective, they have fewer side effects than haloperidol. Several studies have shown good outcomes with sulpiride (Ho et al. 2009; Robertson, Schnieden and Lees 1990). The main side effects are sedation, and sometimes depression. Increased appetite and increased prolactin secretion can also occur.

Atypical neuroleptics

Atypical neuroleptics act by partially blocking the dopamine and serotonin receptors and are often better choices than typical neuroleptics because of reduced side effects. Studies have shown risperidone to be effective, with fewer side effects than haloperidol, although weight gain is a problem (Scahill et al. 2003). Risperidone is also helpful for reducing aggressive behaviour in patients with Tourette syndrome, as well as sleep problems. Other medicines used frequently in the UK are quetiapine (Mukaddes and Abali 2003) and aripiprazole (Yoo, Kim and Kim 2006). Although pimozide is used in Europe and the US, it is not widely used by UK clinicians due to concerns about cardiac side effects.

Noradrenergic agents

Noradrenergic agents such as clonidine, guanfacine and atomoxetine are often useful in children with tics and ADHD symptoms. There are far fewer randomised controlled trials looking at tic reduction with these agents than for the neuroleptics. Nevertheless, studies have shown clonidine, an alpha-2 adrenergic presynaptic agonist can be effective at reducing tics (Leckman *et al.* 1991). Adverse reactions include sedation, headache, dry mouth and sometimes depression. Clonidine also lowers blood pressure and thus monitoring of blood pressure is indicated, and it should not be stopped suddenly as it may result in rapid high blood pressure (rebound hypertension). Guanfacine acts on postsynaptic alpha-2 adrenergic receptors and has been found to be effective in children with tics and ADHD (Scahill *et al.* 2001).

Alternative medication

Tetrabenazine is a vesicular monoamine transporter type 2 inhibitor, which depletes presynaptic dopamine and serotoinin and blocks postsynaptic dopamine receptors. Only a few studies have shown efficacy, and adverse reactions include drowsiness, nausea and some movement disorders (Kenney *et al.* 2007).

Nicotine has been shown to have some effect, either in gum or patch form, although it has been reported as effective in augmenting the effects and benefits of haloperidol (Silver *et al.* 1996). Botulinum toxin injections have been used to treat localised tics, with good effect, particularly in the vocal cords to tackle particularly difficult phonic tics (Porta *et al.* 2004).

Table 6.1 Medications for tic disorders

Neuroleptic medication	Non-neuroleptic medication
Haloperidol	Clonidine
Risperidone	Guanfacine
Sulpiride	Tetrabenazine
Aripiprazole	Nicotine patch
Quetiapin	Botulinum toxin

Treatment of co-occurring conditions in children with tics

There have been long-standing concerns that stimulant medication such as methylphenidate used for children with ADHD may precipitate or worsen tics in some patients. However, this observation alone may not necessarily be a contraindication for its use in TS and co-occuring ADHD, and studies have shown improvement in tics with some children on stimulant medication (Gadow *et al.* 1999; Tourette Syndrome Study Group 2002). The child may benefit enormously if the ADHD symptoms can be reduced. An explanation stating that tics could possibly worsen should be given to the family, and medication should be immediately reviewed if tics do worsen suddenly. Given the natural tendency for tics to wax and wane it is important to monitor the response to medication carefully over a period of several months, unless the tics appear to have a significant impact on the child, and then a decision can be made between the doctor and the family.

A selective serotonin reuptake inhibitor (SSRI) such as fluoxetine or sertraline may be used to target specific OCD symptoms in patients with TS and comorbid OCD.

In summary, caution is required when using medication, but there are a number of studies indicating good improvement with dopamine-blocking medicines and alpha-2 agonists. It is not uncommon for clinicians to use three or four different medicines in succession during the management of a child with particularly difficult chronic tics. The reader is advised to consult recommended national and international guidelines, which are often reviewed and revised in order to offer current advice (see Roessner *et al.* 2011 for European guidelines and Pringsheim *et al.* 2012 for Canadian guidelines).

7

Neurosurgery

From the 1960s onwards, there have been over 30 published reports of surgical intervention for Tourette syndrome. The procedures involve making lesions in parts of the brain. This practice is called 'leucotomy'. Areas chosen include the prefrontal cortex, the limbic area and the thalamus. Like many early surgical procedures on the brain in psychiatry, the studies had limitations in that outcomes were not adequately quantified, and selection did not follow strict criteria and guidelines that could be applied to every case. There were some reported successes but also some very serious complications. It has been difficult to make sense of the studies as broad target areas were chosen for surgical leucotomy.

In the 1970s, a team of physicians reported that nine patients with Tourette syndrome who underwent either unilateral or bilateral ablation of the intralaminar and medial thalamic nuclei reported 50 to 100 per cent reduction in tic frequency (Hassler and Dieckmann 1973). More importantly, there were minimal side effects or complications. The thalamic area of the brain was chosen as it was used in the first studies of deep brain stimulation for Tourette syndrome.

Deep brain stimulation

Deep brain stimulation (DBS) is a form of electromagnetic brain stimulation therapy that uses a pulse generator which provides continuous stimulation of a particular localised area of brain tissue via electrodes that are in contact with a target brain area. As shown in Figure 7.1, DBS involves implanting electrodes via a hole in the skull into a target brain area associated with the basic pathophysiology of a disease. Insertion of the electrodes involves clinical precision and care using neuroimaging and electrophysiological recordings which identify the anatomical boundaries of the target.

Once the electrode is in the correct position, the internal pulse generator is inserted under the skin, usually adjacent to the clavicle (collarbone) in the upper chest. The electric pulse is adjustable and thus can take time to fine-tune to achieve adequate results.

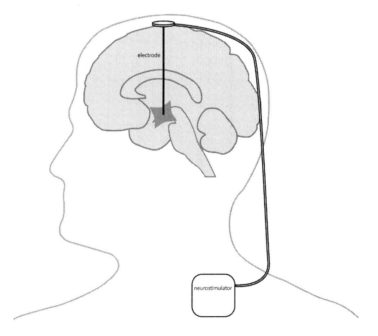

Figure 7.1 Deep brain stimulation

Since the late 1980s, DBS has been widely used to help individuals with chronic Parkinson's disease and other movement disorders with significant success. However, it must be stated that the true mechanism of the treatment remains unknown.

DBS in Tourette syndrome

The success of DBS in individuals with Parkinson's disease resulted from a good understanding of the cause of the disease using clinical expertise, but also from studies in animals (animal models) improving understanding of anatomy and physiology. However, the underlying neural circuitry and physiology is less well understood in Tourette syndrome. The first DBS study in Tourette syndrome was carried out in 1999. The area of the brain targeted was a trajectory involving the centromedian and ventral internal thalamic nuclei and substantia paraventricularis (Vandewalle *et al.* 1999), regions that had been ablated in surgical studies done in the 1960s. It was believed that these areas were involved in setting up a dysfunctional abnormal cortico-striatal-thalamic-cortical circuit involving the basal ganglia and thalamus, leading to increased excitation of the cortex and decreased inhibition of the thalamus. This would lead to a failure to suppress involuntary movements, resulting in tics. Several studies were done by the same team with variable success rates, with tic frequency being reduced by 72 to 90 per cent. The team also found that individuals with Tourette syndrome compulsions also improved (Visser-Vandewalle *et al.* 2003, 2006).

Since 1999 there have been a number of case reports and case series highlighting improvement with surgeons targeting the intralaminar thalamic nuclei and the internal pallidum. At least nine different brain regions have been identified and used in DBS. These targets are part of the ventral striatal basal ganglia, the thalamocortical sensorimotor circuits and the limbic associative circuits thought to be involved in symptoms of Tourette syndrome. The choice of which areas to target depends on the clinician's understanding of the disorder. Some target the sensorimotor areas, as Tourette syndrome is a movement disorder, while others target the limbic area, preferring to see tics as a compulsion or a failure to inhibit them. The majority of studies are case studies, with a handful of studies involving more than one patient.

In 2008, an Italian study reported on 18 patients who underwent DBS involving the thalamic and parafascicular area (Servello *et al.* 2008). Twelve months after DBS there was a 65 per cent improvement in tics.

A Cleveland study in 2007 looked at five patients and found significant reduction in motor and vocal tics following DBS which persisted after three months (Maciunas *et al.* 2007) .

It is very difficult to compare studies due not only to selection criteria and variation in symptoms but also the variation in brain target identified and co-occurring conditions. One also needs to be mindful of the added bias that successful cases get published and reported more frequently than unsuccessful ones.

Complications other than from the surgical procedure itself, such as haematoma and bleeding, include tiredness, hemiparesis (paralysis of one side of the body), depression and psychosis. There are now clear guidelines for clinicians performing DBS (Mink *et al.* 2006; Müller-Vahl *et al.* 2011). Some of the inclusion criteria in the UK are that:

- the individual must be 25 years or older

- the individual has chronic severe tics with functional impairment

- the individual has been treated with adequate dose of medication with poor results.

Exclusion criteria include tics caused by other neurological causes, and any significant psychosocial factors that increase the risk of the procedure, for example a history of non-compliance.

Despite DBS studies being done in nearly 80 patients, DBS is clearly still an experimental procedure requiring strict ethical approval and guidelines. Further studies are needed.

8

Not Yet Validated Treatments

For every family with a child with TS, there is a hope that there will be a cure, or even a treatment that will have a significant and long-lasting impact on the child's tics. Unfortunately, as has been described above, our best-researched and validated treatments tend to only reduce tics by about 30–40 per cent on average for most children.

Many families try a range of treatments. Some families get results after trying many different strategies to reduce their children's tics. Typically, conventional practitioners will suggest that your child tries a treatment that has a proven evidence base. Several interventions are described that have a less well-established evidence base. Please note that this is not an exhaustive list but gives an overview.

Acupuncture

Acupuncture is a treatment which originates from ancient Chinese medicine. It involves the insertion of fine needles into certain sites in the body for therapeutic purposes. Acupuncture is based on the belief that energy flows through the body in channels called meridians, and there is evidence that the treatment can stimulate muscle tissue and nerves under the skin. For people with tic disorders, the goal is to reduce or eliminate tics for the individual. There have been a plethora of studies investigating acupuncture in people with Tourette syndrome during the past 20 years. However, to date, the quality of the studies has been low, and anecdotal clinical reports highlight few benefits from the intervention.

Craniosacral therapy

Craniosacral therapy is a practice that uses very light touch to balance the craniosacral system in the body (the bones, nerves, fluids and connective tissues of the cranium and spinal area). There is little evidence to support this form of intervention in helping with the management of tics. In fact, there have been some cautions about its safety in using it with younger children.

Dental orthotics (dental braces)

The benefits of an oral orthotic device (dental brace) for reducing tic severity in children has had a lot of publicity in recent years but with little or no compelling evidence behind it. The device, known in dentistry as an 'occlusal splint', is a removable mouthpiece typically used for the treatment of temporomandibular joint dysfunction, which is fairly common. The idea is that abnormalities in the temporomandibular joint alignment can cause tics via reflexes of the spinal trigeminal nucleus, without involvement of the brain. There have been reports that wearing dental braces can benefit individuals with chronic tic disorders and reduce tics. In order to answer the question of whether this intervention works with certainty, a clinical trial has been funded by the Tourette Association of America. Fees for the treatment need careful consideration as they can reach up to £10,000 ($15,000).

Physical exercise

Laboratory- and community-based studies suggest that regular exercise can be beneficial for reducing tics. Indeed, regular exercise has been shown to improve mood and anxiety levels in many studies. Studies show that short bouts of exercise such as playing on a Wii Fit for an hour (Liu *et al.* 2011; Nixon *et al.* 2014) or 30 minutes of aerobic exercise (Packer-Hopke and Motta 2014) have some promise in reducing tics and/or improving mood. Our experience of working with children with tics suggests that engaging with some form of exercise such as trampolining, football or even going for a walk after school can be beneficial. However, we need more studies to understand which types of exercise may be particularly beneficial. In general, the exercise should be fun, help your child feel positive about himself and facilitate his ability to manage stress.

Music and focus

Although there is limited research in this area, many people report that their tics reduce when they are playing an instrument or singing. This is not too surprising given that most people's tics reduce when they are focused on an activity. A recent study (Bodeck, Lappe and Evers 2015) showed that a group from Germany reported fewer tics when listening to and/or playing an instrument.

Many people with Tourette syndrome report that focusing on a task such as playing with an adhesive such as Blu-Tack, chewing gum or sucking a boiled sweet can be very helpful, particularly for a tricky vocal tic or a distracting motor tic. For some individuals, tapping a tune gently when they walk or listening to music through earphones can make a big difference.

Nutritional supplements

To our knowledge there is no good scientific evidence that any particular diet or supplement affects tics for better or for worse. A study by Kirsten Müller-Vahl (Müller-Vahl *et al.* 2008) in Germany investigated aspects of the diet of individuals with Tourette syndrome. Findings suggested that caffeine- and/or sugar-containing drinks might worsen tics. There have also been suggestions that magnesium and vitamin B12 should be studied as they may improve tics, but to our knowledge there are no results from the research to date.

Families certainly report that they see some improvement in tics when certain foods are avoided. As long as the child is following a well-balanced diet there should be no problem with excluding some foods to see if this helps.

Conclusion

Parents should be wary of treatments that cost a lot of money, or could potentially cause distress, disappointment or discomfort for the family and/or the child. As a parent you are well placed to consider the available information and decide what treatments are best for your child. It can be very beneficial to discuss your ideas and thoughts with a respected and trusted health professional if you are uncertain, or to evaluate the pros and cons of a treatment.

Part 3

Co-Occurring Features and Conditions

9

Attention Deficit Hyperactivity Disorder

What is attention deficit hyperactivity disorder?

Attention deficit hyperactivity disorder (ADHD) is the most commonly co-occurring condition with Tourette syndrome. ADHD is described as a persistent pattern of inattention and/or hyperactivity-impulsivity that interferes with functioning or development, with difficulties noticed before 12 years of age.

How common is ADHD?

Throughout the world, about 3–10 per cent of children are thought to have ADHD, with lower rates of about 4 per cent in adulthood. It is about two to three times more common in boys than girls.

Characteristics of ADHD

ADHD can present itself as an inattentive type, a hyperactivity/impulsivity type, or a combination of all three symptoms. The key characteristic features are shown in Table 9.1.

Table 9.1 Characteristics of ADHD

Inattention	Hyperactivity	Impulsivity
Careless mistakes	Fidgety	Blurts out answers before questions are completed
Difficulty sustaining attention	Unable to stay seated	
Seems not to listen	Moving excessively	Constantly interrupts conversations
Fails to finish tasks	Noisy in play	
Avoids tasks requiring sustained attention	On the go	Difficulty awaiting turns
Difficulty with organisation	Talks excessively	
Loses things		
Easily distracted		
Forgetful		

A helpful way of seeing children with ADHD is that they have 'leaky brakes', in that the usual controls that most children can put on their behaviour and thinking is a challenge for children with the condition. Difficulties with inattention usually show themselves in a younger child by being bored very easily unless he is involved in a task he very much enjoys, particularly one that involves a computer screen. In the teenage years, the symptoms can appear slightly differently, in that the young person makes unnoticed errors in their work or often appears to be day-dreaming. Hyperactivity also looks different depending on the age of the individual, but the general understanding is that the person appears to always be on the go. The child with ADHD may struggle to sit at the dinner table throughout a full meal or to remain in his seat during a classroom lesson.

The impulsivity element of the condition typically appears to be challenges with being patient. The child with ADHD will probably struggle to wait in a queue or listen to what another person says without interrupting, or he may blurt out the answer in the classroom without thinking to put up his hand.

What causes ADHD?

Both ADHD and TS are caused by the motor and 'braking' (inhibitory) systems in the child's brain maturing more slowly. Many brain regions, both within the structures and the connections between structures (the fronto-striatal-cerebellar circuits), are thought to be involved, and brain imaging studies (Shaw *et al.* 2006) suggest that children with ADHD have slower patterns of maturation than their peers without ADHD, lagging behind by about two years.

ADHD and TS

About 20–30 per cent of children with ADHD also have a tic disorder, and about two-thirds of children with tic disorders will meet the criteria for ADHD.

It is very important to consider both conditions in tandem, although like all neurodevelopmental conditions, ADHD affects people on a spectrum. Many children with mild attention difficulties may not meet diagnosis for ADHD but would benefit from strategies to help them with focus at home and within the classroom. It may be that a child only shows transient mild difficulties in one area (e.g. home and not school), which would be unlikely be diagnosed as ADHD but would certainly be worth discussing with the health professionals involved in the child's care.

Both ADHD and TS run in families and are considered inherited conditions. Twin studies show 50–90 per cent concordance for tic disorders in monozygotic pairs, with about 20 per cent concordance amongst dizygotic twins. Environmental factors may contribute to developing both TS and ADHD, such as smoking during pregnancy, premature birth, complications at birth and low birth weight.

Given that children with both ADHD and TS tend to be very active and move around a lot, it is difficult for clinicians to disentangle ADHD symptoms from tics in children who have both disorders. This may mean that sometimes ADHD is not recognised in a child with tics, and diagnosis involves detailed assessment.

Investigations such as brain scans are rarely needed in the assessment of either TS or ADHD. In some diagnostic centres, testing of attention and hyperactivity is carried out via computer-based tasks.

ADHD symptoms usually appear at an earlier age than tics, in the preschool or early school years. Although it was previously thought that children grow out of ADHD symptoms as they mature into adults, it appears more and more now that about half of all adults will continue to experience ongoing symptoms which can benefit from medication or cognitive behavioural therapy treatments. The way ADHD presents in children with TS does not appear to be any different from the way in which it presents in children with ADHD who do not have TS (Spencer *et al.* 2001).

Management of ADHD

Treatment of ADHD in children with tic disorders is based on a detailed understanding of the impact of symptoms on the child. Ideally, this assessment would include progress at school, emotional function, friendships and family relationships. There are very specific and well-researched treatments for children with ADHD (see National Institute of Clinical Excellence (NICE) 2016) and these are rarely different for children who also have a co-occurring diagnosis of TS.

Evidence shows that treatment of ADHD is very important in ensuring the positive progress of a child with the condition. Most often, treating the ADHD is likely to be the most pressing and beneficial intervention for the child in terms of promoting a positive quality of life and function.

A review of studies in this area demonstrated that learning about each condition (its causes, how symptoms change with time, and how to explain the condition to other people) is an important first step in living with the condition. It has been noted that it is important not only for the child to understand his conditions but also the important people in his life, such as family and teachers. If the symptoms are fairly mild then it may be that this level of intervention is all that is needed. In addition to learning about the symptoms, some children with ADHD and TS will benefit from minor changes in their environment, such as sitting at the front of the classroom, having fiddle toys to play with, and using simple instructions and visual timetables. Above all, structured routines are very important for a child who tends to be impulsive and inattentive, although this can be said for all children generally.

Medication

Medication is a common treatment for children with ADHD, and there has been a significant increase in its use in the western world over the past ten years. The use of some ADHD medications – so-called stimulants – in the treatment of children with tic disorder has been controversial. There was previously a belief that medication could increase or even start tics in children with ADHD. However, studies since the 1980s have shown that stimulants are both effective and safe for ADHD symptoms in patients with tics. The reason for the belief seems to be that tics often start at about six to nine years of age, and this is the most common period for children to be first treated with stimulant medications. Overall, the consensus amongst experienced clinicians is that there is little evidence to suggest that treatment with stimulants (e.g. Ritalin) either causes or significantly increases tics in children. Guidelines from NICE suggest that medication should be used as a short-term treatment, which allows for the possibility to develop new strategies and patterns of behaviour to reduce the negative cycles which may have built up around the child.

Medicines used include stimulants such as methylphenidate (Ritalin) and amphetamine, and non-stimulants such as atomoxetine and clonidine.

Psychological management

Different treatments have been found to be effective at different ages for children with ADHD. For young children up to the end of middle childhood (primary or lower school), the most evidence is found for parent training programmes (e.g. Triple P: Sanders, Mazzucchelli and Studman 2004; Incredible Years: Jones *et al.* 2008; New Forest Parenting Programme: Thompson *et al.* 2009), which give parents skills in knowing how to respond positively to desirable behaviours and disattend to negative or undesirable behaviours. These programmes make good use of reward approaches and highlight the importance of consistency between parents, while making opportunities for the parents and children to spend positive, constructive and engaging periods of time together each week. Although many parents baulk at the term 'parent training', it is not meant in a derogatory sense. In fact, parents of children with ADHD often do require high-level and extremely well-developed parenting skills in addition to a tolerance for frustration and high levels of patience. These qualities can be referred to as 'super-parenting' skills.

It may be difficult for a parent with ADHD to support his child with planning and organisation owing to his own challenges, and this should certainly be discussed with your child's doctor. If you struggle yourself, you should also discuss with your own doctor whether an assessment might be warranted. If treatment is needed this will very probably benefit not only yourself but also your child.

It is also important for the child to receive support within school. Child-centred academic intervention such as peer tutorials and computer-assisted instruction) has a good evidence base and is often offered in addition to support for parents. Of course, the intensity of the intervention will be in response to the level of severity of the symptoms that the child presents with. Should the symptoms be more pronounced at home than at school, perhaps due to higher levels of predictability or structure at school, then perhaps interventions the parents can do will be prioritised. Similarly, if the student with ADHD (and possibly a specific learning disorder) struggles markedly at school then the majority of the support may be needed within the educational context.

There is evidence for cognitive behavioural therapy (CBT), in which an emphasis is placed on changing both thoughts and behaviour, for teenagers and adults with ADHD. The CBT programmes tend to emphasise treatments for promoting strategies to aid sleep, structure in day-to-day life and organisation of goals and lifestyle. At times, it can be difficult to support a teenager with ADHD and there is evidence for support by an ADHD coach, although use of technology such as reminders and prompts from smartphones can be helpful. Recent research (Sukhodolsky *et al.* 2016) has shown that behavioural interventions such as CBT and parent training are effective in helping children manage angry and aggressive behaviour, which is fairly common in children with ADHD and TS.

Conclusion

The most important aspect of any treatment for ADHD is that the child himself, his significant others and teachers need to understand the condition; this information should be provided early on. There is evidence that the earlier the intervention can be put in place, the better likelihood of a positive outcome for the child. It is thought that understanding and intervention reduce the possibility of a vicious circle emerging in which the child's neurodevelopmental difficulties cause his parents or teachers to feel that he is a naughty child, which then influences the adults' behaviour towards the child, and so the child responds. There is good research to say that a combination of medication and behavioural intervention may improve the long-term well-being of a child rather than one single type of intervention alone.

10

Obsessive Compulsive Disorder

What is obsessive compulsive disorder?

Obsessive compulsive disorder (OCD) is a type of anxiety disorder where a person has trouble with frequent obsessions and/or compulsions that cause marked distress.

Obsessions are recurrent and persistent thoughts, images or impulses that are intrusive and in most (but not all) cases, acknowledged by the person who has the obsessions as senseless. Obsessions are generally accompanied by distressing negative emotions, such as fear, disgust, doubt or a feeling of incompleteness.

Compulsions are repetitive, purposeful behaviours, often performed according to certain rules or in a stereotyped fashion so as to neutralise or alleviate the obsessions and negative emotions that accompany them. Compulsions are often observable behaviours (e.g. washing), but can also be mental rituals (e.g. counting).

Common obsessions and compulsions are listed in Table 10.1.

Table 10.1 Common obsessions and compulsions

Obsessions	Compulsions
Contamination	Washing/cleaning
Aggression	Checking
Sexual	Counting
Hoarding	Ordering
Magical thoughts	Arranging
Obsessions about bodily symptoms	Hoarding
Religious	

In order to meet a clinical diagnosis, there needs to be a degree of impairment in terms of time consumed with OCD symptoms (over one hour per day), distress or interference in everyday functioning. In addition, it should be differentiated from other similar disorders and not simply be excessive worries about real problems.

How common is OCD?

It used to be thought that OCD was a condition that affected adults only but studies in the past 15 years have shown that the condition is prevalent in children, occurring in 1 in 100 children. More boys than girls are affected with OCD (two boys to one girl). It has been reported that OCD occurs in 1–3 per cent of the general population (Heyman, Matrix-Cols and Fineberg 2006).

OCD and tic disorders

About one-third of individuals with Tourette syndrome experience recurrent obsessive compulsive symptoms (Khalifa and von Knorring 2005; Leckman *et al.* 1997). There is some suggestion that OCD and tic disorders may share the same genetic underpinnings, and it has been put forward that the best described subgroup in OCD are those individuals with a lifetime history of tic disorders (Diniz *et al.* 2006). Numerous studies suggest that there are qualitative differences between individuals with OCD with tics and those without tics (Hounie *et al.* 2006). Characteristics of tic-related OCD are:

- more common in males than females

- earlier age of onset of tics and OCD symptoms

- poorer level of response to anti-OCD medication

- increased likelihood of family history.

The most common obsessive symptoms include need for symmetry, touching, counting compulsions, ordering and arranging compulsions, and need for exactness (Leckman *et al.* 1997; Worbe *et al.* 2010). OCD symptoms where tics are also present tend to be more responsive to certain medicines, such as antipsychotic medicines, than in OCD without tics. In fact, sometimes it is difficult to tell the difference between a compulsion and a compulsive tic, such as touching another person. Typically, a compulsion is preceded by an uncomfortable and anxiety-provoking thought, whereas this is less likely to be the case with a complex tic, which may be associated with a mild 'just right' or urge sensation.

Differential diagnosis

Assessment can determine whether the child meets the criteria for OCD and also exclude alternative diagnoses. The following conditions should be considered in the differential diagnosis of OCD.

Normal variation

Some obsessions and compulsions are developmentally appropriate, such as bedtime rituals. Two-to-four-year-olds engage in more compulsive type behaviours (repetitive and 'just-right') than older children (Evans *et al.* 1997). In addition, intrusive thoughts and obsessive compulsive behaviours are prevalent in the general population, therefore it is important that assessment has a measure of impairment in it.

Other obsessive compulsive spectrum disorders

Trichotillomania is a condition in which the individual has an impulse and urge to pull out his own hair. It is often associated with significant distress due to stigma and social anxiety. Medical complications include skin irritation and infections. Treatment is difficult but behavioural approaches similar to habit reversal training and acceptance and commitment therapy have been documented to be successful (Woods and Twohig 2008). Medications such as selective serotonin reuptake inhibitors (SSRIs) are used with some success, although recent success has been reported with clomipramine (tricyclic antidepressant), olanzapine (neuroleptic) and naltrexone (opioid antagonist).

Body dysmorphic disorder is an anxiety-related disorder that causes a person to have a distorted view of how he looks. The thoughts are significantly distressing to the extent that they have an impact on daily functioning. Associated symptoms include social phobia, anxiety disorder and sometimes eating disorders. The cause is uncertain, but a history of low self-esteem due to various causes may contribute. Treatment involves CBT and occasionally SSRI medication.

What causes OCD?

OCD was once thought of as a psychological disorder based on unconscious defence mechanisms. However, recent brain imaging and immunological studies indicate that dysfunction in the central nervous system has a role to play in etiology (Rosenberg and Hanna 2000). Structural neuroimaging studies show increased size of the basal ganglia structures in the brain. Regional cerebral blood flow studies demonstrate increased metabolic activity in the prefrontal cortex and basal ganglia. In addition to the neurological evidence, genetic studies have estimated heritability of obsessions and compulsions to be between 26 and 55 per cent (Hudziak *et al.* 2004; Jonnal *et al.* 2000). This evidence points to an interplay between genetic and environmental factors in the development of OCD. For example, perinatal experiences (intrauterine, birth and postnatal) such as prolonged labour are thought to be a risk factor (Vasconcelos *et al*, 2007).

Treatment

Treatment should be considered following diagnosis as evidence suggests that early intervention promotes a more successful outcome. Particularly important in the treatment of pediatric OCD is family involvement. Treatment should be evidence-based and begin at the least intrusive level (Heyman *et al.* 2006; NICE 2005).

Psychoeducation

Psychoeducation is an essential part of treatment. It helps inform the child and family about OCD. The more they know about OCD, the more they feel in control of it. A brief explanation of the biological basis of OCD can help to stop the child being labelled as naughty by the parents and help them to start 'fighting' it together. In some early or mild cases this may be effective and may require no further intervention.

Cognitive behavioural therapy

Cognitive behavioural therapy has been found to be highly effective in treating children with OCD. A good self-help treatment manual such as *Breaking Free from OCD: A CBT Guide for Young People and Their Families* (2008) by Jo Derisley and colleagues describes the stages of CBT for OCD in children. The first step involves psychoeducation (see above) that helps 'externalise' the OCD so that the child can 'boss back' this enemy. The second stage involves finding out about specific obsessions, compulsions, triggers, avoidance behaviours and consequences. A hierarchy of obsessions and compulsions are built; the bottom or least anxiety-provoking can become a target for treatment. The child is then taught to use a technique called exposure with response prevention (ERP), which was described in Chapter 5 in relation to tics. In ERP, the child experiences the feared object, thought or action and then the compulsion or avoidance behaviour is prevented. The child develops a 'toolkit' of cognitive tactics to resist the OCD. These tools include cognitive resistance (bossing back) and self-administered positive reinforcement. Therapy should be dynamic and interactive to encourage confidence and help the child remember the strategies (e.g. using role play and visual aids). It is important to stress that the CBT approach should be collaborative and thus the client should show some motivation to get better.

Medication

Serotonin reuptake inhibitors are the most common pharmacological treatment for OCD. These include tricyclic antidepressants (TCAs) such as clomipramine and SSRIs like fluvoxamine, sertraline and fluoxetine. A meta-analysis of randomised controlled trials in children and adolescents with OCD found clomipramine to be superior to SSRIs. However, encouragingly, the SSRIs were found to be significantly better than placebo and comparably effective (Geller *et al.* 2003).

A recent study found that a combined treatment of CBT and an SSRI was more effective than either CBT or the SSRI alone. CBT and the SSRI were equally effective but were significantly more effective than a placebo (Pediatric OCD Treatment Study (POTS) Team 2004).

Prognosis

Due to the developments in and availability of treatment for children and adolescents with OCD, research into prognosis is slightly dated and may not represent the true outcome of the disorder at this time. However, a nine-year follow-up study did reveal that most individuals with OCD improve over time, and a more recent meta-analysis of long-term outcome studies found that only 41 per cent of patients had full OCD at follow-up (Micali *et al.* 2010; Skoog and Skoog 1999; Stewart *et al.* 2004). Approximately 50 per cent of participants were still receiving treatment and about 50 per cent felt a need for further treatment. A number of factors predict poorer outcome, including earlier age of onset, longer duration of illness, inpatient status, poor response to initial treatment and co-occuring diagnosis (Stewart *et al.* 2004).

11

Depression

What is depression?

Depression is a condition in which one feels sad and miserable, and shows uncharacteristic behaviour. Any of us can feel like this from time to time but if the symptoms persist for more than two weeks then it is considered depression. One can have depressive feelings, depressive behaviour and depressive thoughts. Depressive feelings include feeling sad and fed up. The behaviour includes tearfulness, becoming withdrawn, loss of interest in fun activities or hobbies and occasionally self-harming behaviour such as cutting. Depressive beliefs are usually negative beliefs about oneself or the future. It is typical to have transient symptoms during childhood and adolescence.

How common is depression?

Depressive symptoms are very common in childhood and adolescence, often peaking at the onset of puberty. Ten to 15 per cent of school-aged children show depressed mood at some point in childhood.

What causes depression?

- Genetics: depression runs in families, particularly if there are physical symptoms such as sleep and appetite problems.

- Personality and temperament: children who are shy and slow to adapt to new situations may be predisposed to developing depression.

- The brain: in adults with depression, there is evidence that depressed individuals have abnormalities in neurotransmitters in the brain. The abnormalities relate to the way these neurotransmitters are metabolised.

- Chronic life adversity: early neglect and lack of affection may lead to depression in later life.

- Viral illness: sometimes lack of energy and withdrawal can occur after a viral illness.

- Major life events, such as bereavement or trauma.

Table 11.1 Characteristics of depression

Key features of depression	Associated symptoms
Depressed mood	Reduced concentration
Loss of interest and enjoyment in pleasurable activities and hobbies	Low self-esteem
	Ideas of unworthiness and guilt
Reduced energy, leading to tiredness and decreased activity	Ideas of self-harm or suicide
	Poor sleep
	Decreased appetite

Tourette syndrome and depression

Tourette syndrome itself can be associated with mood disorders. Depression may be a consequence of living with a challenging condition that has a physical and psychological impact. The neurotransmitter dysfunction causing involuntary tics may also cause low mood. A number of drugs used to manage tics can cause depression, especially antipsychotics, but also clonidine.

Studies have shown that depression is prevalent in Tourette syndrome, with about 13 per cent of patients having symptoms that meet diagnostic criteria (Robertson 2006). Some studies suggest that depressive symptoms may moderate the relationship between tic severity and functional impairment in adults with chronic tic disorders (Lewin *et al.* 2011). A recent study showed that the feature of irritability was greater in adults with Tourette syndrome and depression compared to adults with major depression without Tourette syndrome (Carlo, Piedad and Cavanna 2016).

How is depression diagnosed?

Diagnosis requires a detailed history, taking into consideration the duration of depressive symptoms and triggering events. Questioning around feelings, thoughts and behaviour is important. It is often useful to get information on how the child is coping at school. It is important to see if the child is still interested in his or her usual hobbies and interests.

Outcome

If untreated, depressive symptoms may persist, leading to continued low self-esteem and avoidance of school and friends, which then leads to a vicious cycle of feeling more depressed. Serious and persistent low mood could lead to self-harm and suicidal thoughts so it is important for parents not to ignore such symptoms in the hope that they will go away.

Management of depression

The first thing to do is to listen to your child. Talking about worries may be helpful. If possible, help alleviate any particular stresses such as bullying, school problems or family dysfunction. If the symptoms persist, then talk to the school or GP. The school may have a counsellor who could help.

Psychological management
Cognitive behavioural therapy
CBT looks at thoughts (cognitions), feelings and behaviour. It focuses on identifying unhelpful thinking patterns, such as always magnifying the negatives and minimising the positives.

Interpersonal therapy
Interpersonal therapy (IPT) is a short-term therapy that focuses on the interaction between relationships, emotions and mood. This type of therapy may be more appropriate where the mood problems are influenced by the relationships with family members and peers.

Family therapy
Family therapy may be helpful in changing aspects of family interaction, such as conflict, which are associated with onset and continuation of low mood.

Medication

Medication is sometimes used for young people with mood disorders, but it needs to be monitored, as side effects such as self-harming and suicidal behaviour have been reported in young people on certain antidepressants. The most commonly prescribed medicines in the UK include the SSRI medicines such as fluoxetine and sertraline.

12

Anxiety

What is anxiety?

Anxiety is a typical and common part of childhood. It is an emotion which gives the person an unpleasant feeling of tension or apprehension. There are often physical symptoms such as feeling hot, shaking and dry mouth when a child feels anxious. Anxiety often arises as a reaction to some sort of threat or perceived threat, such as a thunderstorm or worries about a parent's health.

Anxiety in childhood will vary according to age with some symptoms increasing or decreasing as the child gets older. In most cases, anxiety in children is temporary, and may be triggered by a specific stressful event.

When anxiety in children is persistent, interferes with normal routines, and doesn't go away with reassurance and comfort, it is classified as an anxiety disorder.

Anxiety disorders in children

There are several types of anxiety disorder, all of which are reasonably common in children with Tourette syndrome:

- Generalised anxiety disorder: these children often have excessive worries about a range of things such as themselves, family and the future. They may have difficulty relaxing and feel restless.

- Separation anxiety disorder: infants often show anxiety when their mother or father leaves the room. This generally develops between eight and 24 months of age, and decreases from 30 months onwards. If symptoms persist by the time the child goes to school, it is described as a disorder. There may be clingy behaviour at school. The child may be worried about something bad happening to them or to their parents. They may refuse to go to school.

- Phobias: children with a phobia have an intense, extreme and irrational fear of something specific, such as dogs, needles or the dark. This often leads to them avoiding situations where they may encounter what they are afraid of.

How common is anxiety?

Anxiety disorders occur in about 2–3 per cent of children.

What causes anxiety?

- Genetics and family: fear is a normal response to a perceived danger. It is important for survival, so infants and children will generally show this. Fear and anxiety levels are predetermined by our genes.

- Learning: children learn that things are frightening and that relief is obtained by avoiding the situation. Escape from the unpleasant situation is thus rewarded by the relief, and more likely to occur in similar situations in the future. Children sometimes learn anxious behaviour by watching their parents' anxiety in certain situations.

- Traumatic situations: any trauma can bring about anxiety, such as bullying, a car crash, bereavement and so on. This makes the child more vulnerable, but a lot will depend on the actual details of the trauma, such as injuries, immediate availability of help and how adults respond to the child and help him to feel safe.

Characteristics of anxiety

Common signs and symptoms of general anxiety in children include:

- worries about a range of subjects, leading to avoidance of situations
- a sense of dread when going out
- palpitations
- feeling panicky
- feeling sick
- feelings of dizziness
- needing reassurance all the time
- using the toilet often
- complaints of stomach aches or headaches
- sleep problems or difficulty concentrating
- behavioural changes such as mood swings, short temper or clinginess
- refusal to go to school or certain places such as shopping centres or parks
- fear of being left alone.

Tourette syndrome and anxiety

Specht *et al.* (2011) looked at patients with chronic tic disorder and found social phobia in 21 per cent, and generalised anxiety in 20 per cent. Other studies have shown higher anxiety symptoms in young people with Tourette syndrome than those without TS. Lewin *et al.* (2011) found that anxiety increased tic severity and functional impairment in adults with chronic tic disorders. Anxiety has also been shown to increase the risk of sleep-related difficulties in children with tics (Storch *et al.* 2009).

How does anxiety relate to tics?

- Anxiety may coexist separately to Tourette syndrome.

- Anxiety may be due to OCD symptoms.

- There may be social anxiety due to the nature of the tics and associated stigma.

- Side effects of antipsychotic medication can sometimes increase agitation and anxiety.

How is anxiety diagnosed?

There is no blood test or biological measurement for anxiety. The diagnosis is made by looking at the intensity and duration of symptoms, usually through asking verbally and also via standardised questionnaires for parents, teachers and the child. Questions are usually about whether the child needs reassurance every day, avoidance of situations, physical symptoms and whether there are repetitive rituals. Observation of the child in certain situations may be helpful.

Outcome

If left untreated, anxiety problems can lead to avoidance, such as school refusal or avoiding social situations, leading to all sorts of problems. Anxiety symptoms may persist into adulthood or lead to mood problems such as depression.

Management of anxiety

There are several things that a parent can do to reduce anxiety:

- Listen to your child and encourage him or her to talk about fears and thoughts.

- Be a role model and show your child how you deal with similar situations.

- Lots of preparation, such as planning when and where you go out so you know about toilets, meeting points, travel times, etc.

- Try to keep the house as peaceful as possible.

- Continue to enjoy things together, such as games, movies, etc.

- Keep to familiar routines, such as bedtimes and homework times, etc.

- Physical activity is important to regulate blood pressure, so exercise and sports will help. If the anxiety symptoms persist then consult your doctor.

There are a range of therapies that may help. Talking therapies such as CBT use a range of techniques such as:

- Psychoeducation: teaching the young person about the body and understanding the physical symptoms so he realises that the symptoms are natural and part of the emotion.

- Cognitive restructuring: this is where the young person is taught to rethink his worries. For example, a child may think that all school buses crash. The child is helped to see that this is not a true statement and that buses are safe with safe procedures. Also, if a bus did crash there are things that would keep the child safe such as seatbelts, the structure of the bus and so on.

- Exposure with response prevention: this allows the safe exposure of the child to the feared situation in a gradual step-by-step manner. For example, if someone is scared of house spiders, the therapist gets the child to overcome his or her fear by looking at a picture of a house spider until the anxiety has gone. Once this is achieved, the child then has to overcome the next step in the anxiety hierarchy, such as looking at a dead house spider, and so on until the child can cope with looking at a live spider. ERP can be used in a range of situations and is very effective.

Medication does not cure anxiety; it only relieves the symptoms, but it can allow the young person to function at a reasonable level in school or social settings. Medicines for anxiety include SSRI types of medicines such as sertraline and fluoxetine.

13

Autism Spectrum Disorder

Autism spectrum disorder (ASD) is a developmental disorder (or condition) with impairment of a child's ability to interact and communicate socially.

How common is ASD?

According to the latest research, one out of every hundred people will have an ASD.

What causes ASD?

Despite ongoing research, it is not clear what causes ASD. There may not be a single cause and as with Tourette syndrome, multiple genes may be involved resulting in ASD features.

Characteristics of ASD

The characteristics of ASD vary from individual to individual, with a range of severities of presentation. People with ASD have what is usually described as a triad of impairments:

- difficulty with social interaction

- difficulty with social communication

- restricted and repetitive stereotyped behaviour.

Table 13.1 Characteristics of ASDs

Social interaction	Communication	Ritualised, repetitive, restricted pattern of behaviour
Limited eye contact	Lack of non-verbal gestures	Unusual preoccupations
Not wanting to share	Lack of social chat	Interests that are appropriate but occupy significant amount of time
Lack of seeking enjoyment with others	Limited reciprocal conversations	
Not interested in peer group	Inappropriate comments/ questions	Verbal rituals
Lack of interest in others	Echolalia	Resistant to changes to routine
Lack of social smiling		Hand flapping and characteristic finger movements
Poor empathy		Excessive sensory difficulties

Parents may be alerted or become concerned when a young child fails to develop speech at the expected age or is difficult to engage with socially. Not all children with autism are slow to speak. In fact, some speak quite early, and may have a very large and sophisticated vocabulary or an unusually quaint way of speaking. They may appear different to their peers and not always use their language in a flexible communicative manner.

A person with ASD does not always understand the rules of typical social interaction, has difficulty in making friends and may have a love for routines. Other behaviours may be noticed, such as poor eye contact, preference for solitary and repetitive play, distress with change, and unusual interests. Other associated difficulties are oversensitivity to noise, smells, tastes and textures. Some children with ASD can also have additional learning and behavioural difficulties.

Asperger syndrome

'Asperger syndrome' is a term which was used previously but is no longer a term 'officially' used by the medical profession (American Psychiatric Association 2013). Asperger syndrome describes a form of ASD with the same triad of impairments, but there is usually no intellectual challenge or delayed language development, although there may be specific learning disorders such as dyslexia. Formal language ability in this syndrome is not only within the typical range but also tends to be better than the other skills.

People with Asperger syndrome tend to be more aware of their difficulty in understanding the rules of social interaction and, as such, may become anxious and confused.

Tourette syndrome and ASD

There are some subtle similarities in symptom profile when looking at ASD and Tourette syndrome. Both conditions have:

- movement features: ASD patients present with stereotypies (repetitive, ritualistic and rhythmical movements)

- speech abnormalities such as echolalia or palilalia (involuntary repetition of words, phrases or sentences)

- excessive sensory abnormalities
- co-occuring obsessive symptoms.

The prevalence rates of Tourette syndrome and ASD have been looked at in a number of studies. Baron-Cohen *et al.* (1999) identified 8 per cent of children with autism as having co-occuring Tourette syndrome. Canitano and Vivanti (2007) found that 22 per cent of children with ASD in a clinic setting had a tic disorder. Burd *et al.* (2009) looked at a large cohort of individuals with Tourette syndrome and found 4.6 per cent had co-occuring ASD.

Managing children and young people with ASD

Once a diagnosis is made and the profile of a child's needs is clearer, most of the intervention is geared towards ensuring that the child is educated in a suitable school and that difficult behaviours are appropriately managed.

14

Specific Learning Difficulties

Most children with tics and Tourette syndrome have learning skills and make academic progress at a similar level to their peers. The majority of children will not need support above and beyond that described in Part 2, which mainly focuses on strategies to help with understanding tics. However, there are a group of children (probably about 30 per cent as reported by Burd *et al.* 2005) with Tourette syndrome who also have a co-occurring specific learning disorder with reading, writing or maths. In addition, other neurodevelopmental conditions which can affect learning are difficulties with motor skills or language.

It is important to remember, as found in a Norwegian study (Jensen and Steinhausen 2015), that if a child has one neurodevelopmental condition, such as ADHD, then there is a one-in-three chance that they will also have a second condition and a one-in-four chance of having two additional conditions. One of the conditions could include a specific learning disorder. If you have concerns about your child's learning then the first action should be to discuss your concerns with your child's teacher who will probably have similar concerns and will have additional information on the child's attention, application to work and motivation as compared with children of a similar age.

Learning disorders tend to run in families, therefore if you or your child's other parent has or had learning challenges there is a chance that these traits may have been passed on alongside the strengths you see in your child.

Impairment in reading/dyslexia

The most commonly diagnosed and researched form of learning disorder is dyslexia, or reading disorder. Thought to affect about 8–10 per cent of the population, dyslexia is a spectrum disorder, with about 5 per cent of children having a severe form and about 10 per cent coping with a mild form.

Although children struggle to read and spell, the main underlying problem is with processing sounds accurately, referred to as phonological processing. There are other areas of difficulty often found in children with dyslexia, such as slow naming and reading skills and challenges with active short-term memory. The vulnerabilities are only considered dyslexia if a child has had sufficient instruction in phonics and other reading skills and has persistent difficulties with reading. If a child has difficulties with reading there is a strong chance that they will also experience poor spelling. Importantly, a child with severe dyslexia may also experience challenges with understanding text due to struggles decoding a sufficient number of words to comprehend the text. This sort of difficulty is not seen as often in children with mild dyslexia, particularly if their vocabulary is strong.

Sometimes difficulties with reading can be attributable to low motivation, attention challenges or poor teaching. It may be that a child with eye tics struggles to read fluently while he has the bothersome tics, but this is unlikely to affect them over time and we have no reason to think that a child's tics should influence how they learn sounds or learn to read accurately.

There are very well-supported intervention programmes for children with dyslexia. The programmes typically focus on enriching or teaching the child to process sounds (phonics) more accurately. Ideally, these skills should be supported both at home and school. If you have concerns, it would be helpful to discuss with your child's class teacher or the specialist learning teacher in their school.

Impairment in written expression (dysgraphia)

A less well-known and researched learning disorder, dysgraphia or learning disorder with impairment in written language, is also common in children with Tourette syndrome. This may be due to challenges with planning and organisation of writing. It may be that the child is able to effectively use motor skills and do everyday tasks such as doing buttons, tying laces and using cutlery but struggles to produce well-formed, legible handwriting.

There are sensible programmes available to support a child in improving spelling. For younger children, a focus on sounds and the association between the form of the letter (grapheme) and the sounds used to make the word (phoneme) is important. As children grow older, an appreciation of the structure and form of words will be important, such as use of morphemes and compound words. As English is a highly irregular language, children mastering these skills may take longer than children learning more transparent and regular languages such as Spanish or Italian. Learning how to structure sentences and then essays is incredibly important as children move through school. There are several helpful programmes to aid a child with learning to structure sentences and also essays. Details of such programmes can be found in Harris *et al.* (2010) and Moody (2004).

Impairment in maths (dyscalculia)

Difficulties with numbers and maths reasoning are less well understood than literacy disorders but also thought to be fairly common. Children with Tourette syndrome who also have an attention disorder are most at risk for difficulties with numbers. Huckeba and colleagues (2008) found that the difficulties with maths for children with Tourette syndrome appeared in part from making procedural errors in the work.

Difficulties concentrating, abstraction or an underlying difficulty with manipulation and reasoning with numbers may also be at play and it is certainly worth having a discussion with the classroom teacher and if needed, a formal assessment, should concerns persist. Once again, there are supports and interventions to facilitate the development of maths concepts in children. It is helpful to initiate an awareness of numbers and numerical relationships in your child early on so that these can be built on over time. An important note to highlight from recent research is evidence that a child's belief that he can 'do maths' and work with numbers is strongly predictive of their competency with numeracy (Boaler 2010). Therefore, highlighting to your child that everyone has to learn maths and no one is naturally 'just great' at working with numbers may be beneficial.

Developmental motor coordination (dyspraxia)

The term 'praxia' comes from the Latin for 'movement' and dyspraxia refers to difficulty with movement. This may be fine motor skills which use muscles such as those in the hands, or gross motor skills involving muscles such as the legs. Typically, children with dyspraxia show challenges with motor skills early on and challenges with visual planning and organisation as they get older.

Like all of the neurodevelopmental disorders discussed in this book, dyspraxia is a spectrum disorder, with some children having very mild challenges, which may not even require treatment, whereas other children will grow into adults who will continue to manage motor difficulties. Each child with the condition will be different and the diagnostic criteria can be varied depending on the assessment used to make the diagnosis. A child with dyspraxia may take a little longer to walk or talk than his peers. They may be clumsy or struggle to negotiate right and left or to read the time on an analogue clock. As tics heavily involve the motor system, children with Tourette syndrome are at a greater risk for having dyspraxia than their peers without the disorder. Similarly, there are higher rates of children with Tourette syndrome and stuttering than in typically developing children.

In terms of intervention, if you or your child's teacher suspects your child has major and persistent concerns with motor skills then discuss the possibility of a referral to an occupational therapist with them. Occupational therapists are trained to carefully assess and support the development of everyday activities in a child's day-to-day life.

Specific language impairment/ language disorder

Persistent and impairing difficulties with expression and understanding of language are referred to as specific language impairment (SLI) or language disorder. This form of learning difficulty is fairly common, particularly in preschool children, and is thought to occur in about 3 per cent of the school-age population. Children with SLI will likely have experienced long-standing difficulties with early language development which did not progress at a level similar to their peers even with specialist intervention from a speech and language therapist. Having an unrecognised and untreated SLI may impact on the child's social, and subsequently emotional, function. Unsurprisingly, children with SLI can also experience considerable challenges with written language.

A parent with concerns about their child's ability to express themselves through language or understand what other people say should consult their GP or their child's teachers. The professional will, it is hoped, facilitate a referral to a speech and language therapist with specialist knowledge of assessing and treating children's language skills. Should a diagnosis be made it is very helpful for the parents and teachers involved to have a good understanding of the condition and its treatment so that they can practise the skills used by the therapist in day-to-day life.

Specific language impairment often occurs in families, and affected parents should not be afraid of considering how they can improve their confidence in their own vocabulary or ability to construct language. For teenagers with the disorder, it is very helpful to understand that their difficulties with language are not because they are not able, but that, like any weakness, they need tools and training to make progress. Self-guided reading can be helpful in this area and the books recommended in Useful Resources and Websites for both children and their parents are likely to be beneficial.

Processing speed difficulties

Processing speed refers to completing tasks in an efficient manner. Processing speed difficulties are common in children with co-occurring ADHD and Tourette syndrome. Ellen Braaten (Braaten and Willoughby 2014) estimates that approximately 60 per cent of children with ADHD have difficulties with processing visual and verbal information at a speed similar to their peers. Challenges with working as quickly as peers can impact on a child's sense of effectiveness and his ability to complete tasks fluently at home and school.

An assessment by a psychologist or occupational therapist may help in understanding how a child's processing of information impacts on their function. Slow processing speed is not considered a specific disorder in itself but often co-occurs with other learning difficulties, especially dyspraxia. Sometimes processing speed difficulties may occur independently or alongside difficulties understanding information more generally, known as an intellectual disability, which we will discuss later on in this chapter.

Braaten and Willoughby (2014) have proposed three important strategies for children with processing speed difficulties: accepting the challenges; accommodating the difficulties, perhaps through allowing additional time for tasks; and advocating for themselves so that they are able to cope well and achieve their potential. In this way the child should be equipped with the tools to deal with his challenges.

Executive function

One of the areas of thinking that has been most researched in children with Tourette syndrome is executive function. This umbrella term refers to a group of behaviours that facilitate tasks and independence. Such behaviours include organisational and planning skills, task initiation and completion, the ability to keep information in mind as it is being used (so-called working memory) and regulating emotional responses in situations. There is plenty of research and anecdotal evidence to show that these behaviours develop and become more sophisticated and complex as a child grows.

Children with Tourette syndrome and co-occurring ADHD are at risk of markedly slower progress, which naturally can impact on many areas of life, in particular everyday tasks such as completing homework, getting dressed independently and organising school bags. The transition from the highly organised, often single-classroom-based context of primary school to the organisationally demanding environment of secondary or middle school can place considerable stress on the child with executive function demands.

Each area of executive function will benefit from its own type of particular intervention. Approaches can be implemented successfully at home and school; a few are described in Table 14.1.

Table 14.1 Strategies for executive function issues

Area of executive function	Strategy
Organisation	Prompts and reminders from teachers
	Good demonstration of planning by others
	Discussion of plans during meals/start of the day
Planning	Reminders on phone
	Mind maps
Working memory	Clear, well-placed instructions that build on previous consolidated knowledge can help a child develop strategies to complete tasks
	Note taking
	Having teachers/parents repeat instructions
Self-monitoring and work completion	Visual planners
	Timetables and charts
Motivation	Use of reward
	Regular review of an agreed contract with clear targets

Intellectual disability

About 1 per cent of individuals will have learning and independence challenges globally. This level of difficulty is referred to as an intellectual disability and can be experienced at a mild, moderate or severe level. Typically, psychologists will give this diagnosis based on the child's performance on a measure of intellectual function (such as the Wechsler Intelligence Scale for Children – Fifth Edition; Wechsler *et al.* 2014) and reported daily living skills.

The diagnosis is considered when the child struggles in all areas at a level well below his peers. It is very important that a child with Tourette syndrome and intellectual disability is very well supported educationally with a differentiated curriculum, which may be best offered within a special educational environment.

If you do have concerns about any area of your child's progress and he appears to be making slower progress than his peers, then speak with his teacher, the special educational needs co-ordinator or his GP or paediatrician for further information.

15

Sleep

Sleeping well helps to maintain a number of brain functions, including memory and concentration. Table 15.1 shows how much sleep children need every day according to their age group.

Table 15.1 Sleep requirements in children

Age	0–3 months	3–12 months	1–3 years	3–6 years	6–12 years	12 years plus
Average sleep needed in 24 hours	16–20 hours	14 hours	12–14 hours	11–12 hours	10 hours	9–10 hours

Tourette syndrome and sleep

A number of sleep-related problems have been identified in children with Tourette syndrome, but most of the studies have focused on adults, not children. Studies in children with Tourette syndrome have shown poor sleep efficiency, frequent arousal, increased talking, increase in non-tic movements, increased wakenings, walking in sleep and increased reported nightmares (Kostanecka-Endress et al. 2003; Sacconai et al. 2005). Difficulty getting off to sleep was reported more than in the non-clinical population. A study by Storch et al. (2009) demonstrated that 80 per cent of children with Tourette syndrome experience at least one sleep-related problem, with 20 per cent experiencing four or more sleep-related problems. These problems include insomnia, nightmares and refusal to sleep on their own. This finding is not surprising as there is a high percentage of sleep problems in children with neurodevelopmental or psychiatric difficulties. Anxiety may contribute to sleep difficulties, and associated ADHD will also contribute to difficulty getting off to sleep. The authors of the above study speculate that sleep problems may also be related to high levels of stress resulting from increased fatigue.

Unlike in adults with Tourette syndrome, Storch *et al.* (2009) did not find a correlation between tic severity and sleep problems. In some cases, children with severe motor tics slept better, which may be due to exhaustion.

Polysomnography, the study of sleep using EEG to look at brain waves and patterns when asleep, shows that children with Tourette syndrome have markedly altered sleep quality and difficulty getting off to sleep and maintaining sleep. Sleep problems in children with Tourette syndrome include:

- difficulty falling asleep
- frequent waking at night
- difficulty getting back to sleep
- sleep walking
- sleep talking
- nightmares
- increased non-tic movements
- separation anxiety
- refusal to sleep on their own.

Sleep loss may impair basic brain function, leading to poor control of complex behaviour, and problems with attention and regulation of emotions. The combination of disturbed sleep, increased arousal and reduced ability for motor inhibition may increase the likelihood of tics.

Sleep problems increase in children with co-occurring conditions such as ADHD and anxiety. If your child with Tourette syndrome also has ADHD, then remember that one of the side effects of stimulant medication is difficulty getting off to sleep. ADHD has also been found to be linked to other sleep-related problems, including restless leg syndrome (restless sleep and repetitive kicking movements) and obstructive sleep apnoea (loud snoring, restless sleep and breathing difficulties). Migraine, which can be caused by tics, may also contribute to sleep problems.

It is not surprising that lack of sleep leads to problems, which can include:

- poor memory and concentration leading to problems at school

- anxiety

- behaviour problems including aggression and tantrums

- irritability

- increased stress in other family members due to disturbance at night.

Management
Practical measures to improve sleep
At first you can try simple tips to improve your child's sleep and if they are not effective, you should see your child's doctor for further assessment and treatment.

- Encourage your child to do regular exercise and activities during the daytime.

- Avoid food or drinks containing caffeine such as chocolate, coffee, tea or cola in the late afternoon or evening (within six hours of going to sleep).

- Avoid vigorous and stimulating activities one to two hours before bedtime, such as watching TV or playing computer games. Unfortunately, we are in the age of social media and many children have their phones/tablets/laptops next to them when they sleep (as do adults – we need to set an example!).

- Your child's bedroom should be dark, safe, comfortable and cosy.

- Keep a bedtime routine and ensure bedtime and wake-up times are the same each day during school days. We are happy to say that holiday time can be more relaxed, but be prepared to increase the routine as you get closer to the school term starting again, particularly after the long summer vacation.

If your child has significant bedtime or night-time anxiety then discuss with your doctor about referral to a psychologist for help with anxiety.

Medication

Some medicines used to manage Tourette syndrome can help with sedation. Risperidone and clonidine both have sedative effects which may be useful when prescribed to be taken at night. Occasionally other medication may be useful for sleep problems. In the UK, melatonin is widely used. It is available as a tablet and liquid and has been prescribed widely in clinics for children with ADHD and autism. Melatonin is a natural hormone produced by the pineal gland in the brain which helps to initiate sleep. It is found in foods such as rice, oats, barley, ginger, sweetcorn and tomatoes. Despite this, it can only be prescribed by a doctor and is not available over the counter in pharmacies. It is always helpful to ensure that a regular bedtime routine and the other approaches listed above have been tried before medication is sought.

16

Anger

Tourette syndrome and aggression

Studies have shown that 37 per cent of patients with Tourette syndrome report anger-control problems at some point (Freeman *et al.* 2000). In a Swedish school study, teachers rated 35 per cent of children with Tourette syndrome as having problems with aggression (Kadesjo and Gillberg 2000). Anger in children with Tourette syndrome:

- is usually sudden

- rapidly rises to a peak

- may bring relief after an episode

- may be related to low mood

- tends to occur in those who are inflexible and rigid in their thinking

- occurs when tired

- may be related to feeling frustrated or embarrassed.

Aggression is often the reason a child with Tourette syndrome is referred for clinical care. For most children with Tourette syndrome, the anger outbursts tend to occur three to four times a week. Aggressive behaviour has been shown to be increased in children with ADHD, primarily because of impulsive behaviour. It is also increased in anxiety disorders including obsessive compulsive disorders, possibly as a result of anxiety and discomfort leading to frustration. Figure 16.1, as illustrated by a child with ADHD, shows the association between anger and tics.

I feel angry when I have tics, crocodiles can be aggressive and angry, this is why I have chosen a crocodile.

Figure 16.1 Anger and tics

Explosive outbursts

Explosive outbursts, also known as rage attacks, are severe impulsive episodes of anger. The onset is often in childhood, leading to significant behavioural problems both at home and school. A 'rage attack' is not a 'temper tantrum'. Tantrums are usually goal-directed, that is, their purpose is to get someone to do something you want. With 'rage' attacks, the goal appears to be a release of tension that has been building up.

Between 23 and 40 per cent of children with Tourette syndrome report problems of this kind, however it is likely to be related to co-occurring problems such as ADHD and anxiety and not specific to Tourette syndrome (Wright, Rickards and Cavanna 2012). The rage attacks often occur with no provocation or trigger, or may be disproportionate to the trigger. They may be preceded by increased arousal.

Figure 16.2 shows anger symptoms as described by a group of children with Tourette syndrome.

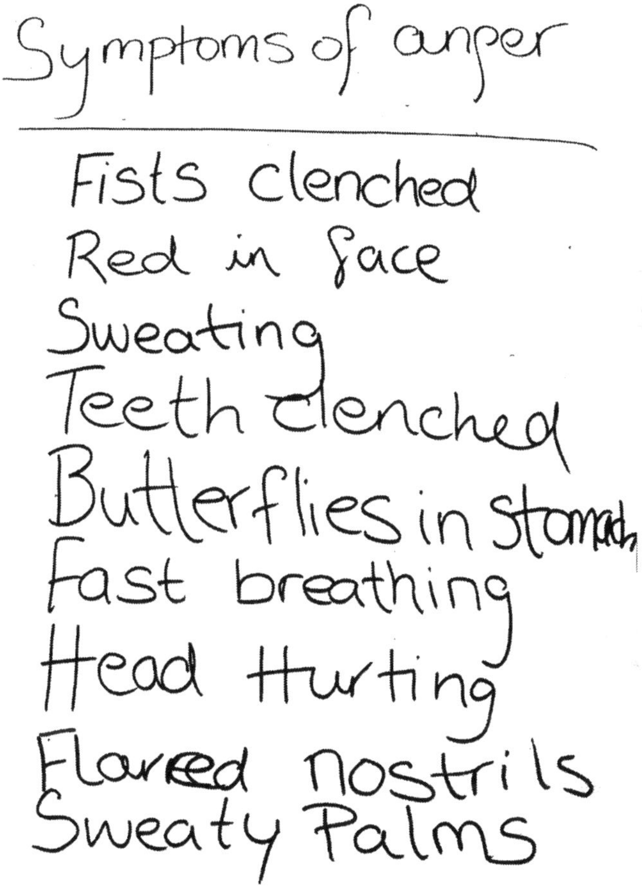

Symptoms of anger

Fists clenched
Red in face
Sweating
Teeth clenched
Butterflies in stomach
Fast breathing
Head Hurting
Flared nostrils
Sweaty Palms

Figure 16.2 Symptoms of anger

After the event, there is often remorse or shame, which distinguishes this rage from the lack of empathy in other conditions. There may also be a sense of relief and calmness after the rage episode. Figure 16.3 shows how a child compared their experience of rage to a dragon.

Figure 16.3 Rage

Self-injurious behaviour

Self-injurious behaviour (SIB) is deliberate repetitive behaviour causing harm to oneself that occurs without suicidal intent. The behaviours occur in a small group of children with Tourette syndrome and appear to be increased in children with greater tic severity. The SIB tends to increase if the child has co-occurring conditions. Self-directed injuries include pinching, slapping, biting, head banging and hitting oneself. One study has shown that symptom severity correlates with the presence of obsessive compulsive symptoms (Mathews *et al.* 2004). There is a correlation with episodic rage and increased risk-taking behaviour. SIBs are also reported in many people with co-occuring ADHD.

Psychological management

Anyone can become angry – that is easy. But to be angry with the right person, to the right degree, at the right time, for the right purpose and in the right way – this is not easy.

Aristotle

The premise of anger management involves learning about the function of anger and its effect on the individual and people around them. It is important to see anger as a reaction to a threat in which the body prepares itself for 'flight' or 'fight'. This is a biological automatic response. Anger is the choice of 'fight'. The list shown in Figure 16.4 was offered by a group of children with Tourette syndrome who described their anger as a volcano erupting.

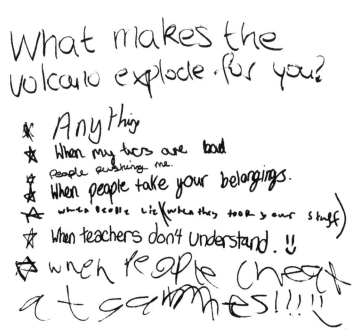

Figure 16.4 Anger as a volcano

Anger is often a secondary emotion; the primary emotion may be feelings of rejection or self-rejection, fear, embarrassment, disappointment or frustration. Recognising this and learning to deal with the primary emotion is key to anger management.

We handle anger in different ways, such as:

- burying it (repressed anger, where the person is not conscious of the anger)

- choosing not to express it, or being unable to express it (suppressed anger)

- taking it out on someone else (displaced anger)

- expressing the anger, but badly (problem anger)

- expressing it properly (normal anger).

Again, recognising how we express anger is important. There are a number of helpful ways you can deal with anger:

- be curious about your feelings

- move away

- do something different

- really listen

- ignore it

- control your thoughts

- exercise

- talk to friends who you like and who make you feel good.

If you feel yourself getting angry with someone, before you speak to the other person, try relaxing tense muscles or clenched fists, make space between you and the person, and breathe slowly. This gives you space to think through what you may say next. Again, ideas from a group of children with Tourette syndrome and anger symptoms are shown in Figure 16.5.

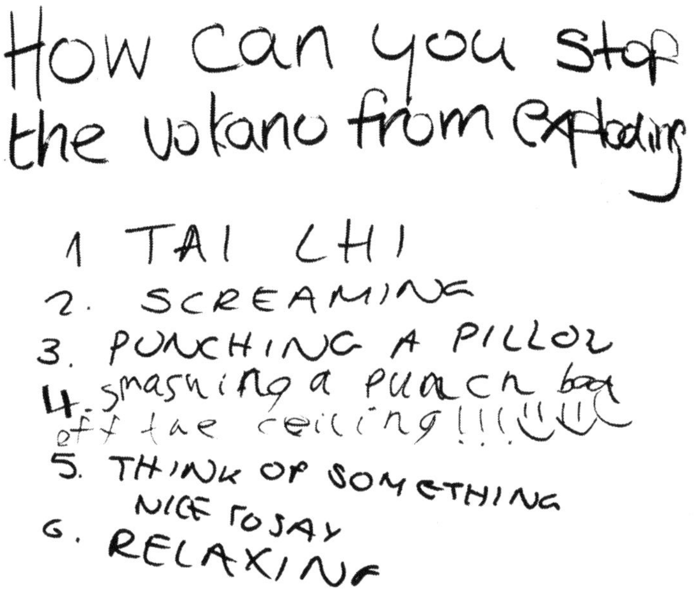

How can you stop
the volcano from exploding

1 TAI CHI
2. SCREAMING
3. PUNCHING A PILLOW
4. smashing a punch bag
   off the ceiling!!!!!
5. THINK OF SOMETHING
     NICE TO SAY
6. RELAXING

Figure 16.5 Controlling the volcano

Tips for parents

- Identify triggers or situations that make things worse.

- Keep things positive and remember to praise whenever you see good things (but keep it genuine).

- Try to reduce the negative impact of tics, such as by dealing with issues in school.

- Make time for relaxation.

- Be a good role model in terms of controlling your own anger and temper.

- Leave time for anger to pass away.

- Avoid getting into debates and punitive behaviour when the anger is happening.

- When things are calmer, talk to your child about feelings and other ways of expressing oneself.

- Give good old-fashioned love and hugs.

- Encourage good sleep patterns.

- Keep an eye on education and learning, and show your child that it is important to learn well and to respect teachers.

- Give the child some responsibility as they get older.

- Cultivate interests and individual differences between siblings.

- Encourage sporting activities, as they help release energy but also help with self-esteem.

- Keep an eye on diet habits and don't allow too much junk food, which is often sugar-loaded and can increase irritability and mood problems.

- You have a child with a challenging condition but you know your child better than anyone else. Tap into the positive experiences and your role as a parent to look after and raise your child as best as you can.

- Above all, look after yourself. You are faced with many challenges and other people are quick to give you advice and make you feel inadequate. Be aware of this and remind yourself that you are doing the best you can.

Medication

Medicines used to treat Tourette syndrome can often have calming and sedative effects. The antipsychotics such as risperidone, haloperidol and ariprazole have all been used to help with tics and aggression.

Treatment of co-occuring symptoms may help, such as using SSRIs for OCD and anxiety, and stimulant medication for ADHD.

Part 4

Parenting and Family Life

17

Adjusting to the Diagnosis

Once a diagnosis of Tourette syndrome has been made, parents are likely to experience a range of emotions, including anger, relief, worry, denial, sadness and guilt. There is no 'correct' way in which to react. Everyone reacts differently in his or her own individual way.

Even when parents are sure their child has Tourette syndrome and are expecting confirmation of the diagnosis from a professional, some degree of anxiety takes hold as parents contemplate a future of trying to protect their child after a diagnosis has been confirmed. Some parents see their child very differently from before the diagnosis and go through a period of grief for the loss of the 'perfect child' that they were expecting. Some parents may find it hard to accept the diagnosis and might seek a second opinion.

It is not unusual for parents to feel angry with professionals, particularly if they have seen several professionals in the past who had put the problems down to 'parenting issues', early experiences or school stressors. Parents may start to have worries that their child is going to be bullied, be unable to hold a job or to have an adult relationship, and will face a challenging life. If parents do feel any of the above, it is a perfectly normal reaction provided it is short-lived and they can reconcile these feelings.

All these emotions take time to work through. The majority of parents will deal with these feelings and adjust and successfully adapt in their own time. Once parents start talking to other parents in a similar position and start to read sensible information about Tourette syndrome, they will feel much more confident and reassured. Children certainly do not want their parents worrying all the time or watching them and analysing every situation and tic. In our experience, children respond better if their parents have a positive approach to problems, including a positive approach to dealing with tics.

Guilt

Many parents of children with Tourette syndrome feel guilty about their children's condition and behaviour. They may have been told by others that it is their fault that their child behaves in such a 'naughty' way. People automatically assume parents are at fault if they see a child who is acting differently to his peers.

Many parents feel guilty since they may have punished their child for 'ticcing', thinking that the child was deliberately making faces or noises to annoy his parents. Parents may have shouted at the child, taken pocket money away or grounded their child. Parents should not feel too guilty as this is very common and often a part of the process of developing an understanding of the condition.

Parents may also feel guilty because they have read that genes are passed on to children. Occasionally a parent may blame his or her partner for passing on the 'Tourette' gene. Well, to start with, no one has yet found a specific gene that is passed down in Tourette syndrome. One also forgets that children also inherit from their parents other personality traits such as kindness, patience, thoughtfulness and intelligence, so it is not a simple situation.

We feel that parents who also have the condition know what it is like to live with and cope with Tourette syndrome and so, in fact, are in a better position than most to give good advice to their child on how to cope and what to look out for. They are also able to empathise with their child, which will help with self-esteem. It may be that parents with ADHD, OCD or Tourette syndrome also have a lower threshold for tolerating the symptoms and will have to work especially hard to cope with feelings of frustration around the symptoms themselves. Working as part of a team with co-parents, teachers and other family members is helpful for this.

The basic message is that all children perform better and are better adjusted when their parents are supportive and strong, and not self-absorbed in their own guilt.

Moving on

Accepting and adapting to a child's diagnosis of Tourette syndrome takes time. Acceptance does not happen overnight. Talking to people who have been through similar experiences can help. Seeking support from a local Tourette syndrome group or charity can be valuable. Learn as much as one can about the condition via books and journals. Knowledge is empowerment. In time, parents will learn that Tourette syndrome is not as bad as previously imagined. Because of some of the bizarre and colourful symptoms seen in a minority of cases, the media portrayal and public perception of the condition is at times inaccurate. The more parents know about the condition, the more they will feel in control. However, parents must access information at their own pace. They should not let the condition dominate and take over their lives. With a bit of reading, parents are helpfully likely to become experts in Tourette syndrome. They will probably know more about it than their doctor. It is not uncommon to hear that parents frequently educate their doctors on the condition. The family doctor is likely to be extremely busy and needs to know about many areas of medicine, so any up-to-date information on Tourette syndrome is usually gratefully welcomed. This information may one day help other children to get an earlier diagnosis and receive appropriate management.

Siblings

Once again, different people react in different ways. If a child has Tourette syndrome, it is likely that his or her siblings will be aware of the symptoms and may be affected by their behaviour. This is probably more so if the child also has features of ADHD or severe OCD. The sibling may feel annoyed by the vocal tics. They may feel that parents give more attention to their sibling. There is a need to minimise any resentment building up amongst siblings. The sibling should not miss out on any special events because of his or her sibling's Tourette syndrome or associated difficulties. A common example of this is a day trip being cut short and the whole family returning early due to a child's 'difficult' behaviour.

Parents should explain Tourette syndrome to the sibling. Sometimes we explain to young children that tics are like 'hiccups in the brain'. Siblings should also be reminded that the noises their brother or sister makes cannot be controlled.

Parents may need to give special time to the sibling since the child with Tourette syndrome will take up an enormous amount of the parents' time. In some cases, the sibling may also feel left out since his or her brother or sister gets special attention from doctors and teachers.

Relatives

Most family members will be keen to understand about the child and their Tourette syndrome. Parents can provide relatives with information and fact sheets on the condition. However, there may be some members of the family who refuse to accept the diagnosis through ignorance, denial or other reasons. Many parents feel let down by some of the attitudes of family members and this sometimes hurts more than anything else. Parents should not expect that everyone will be sympathetic and understanding.

Parents may have to continuously remind certain relatives of the nature of tics. If, after trying to explain a child's condition, parents are still met with scepticism and disapproval, then the parents have to consider whether their child is suffering or experiencing any difficulties when in the company of these relatives. Many relatives are often at a loss to know what they can do to help but there are some simple strategies which can help, such as:

- Provide the relative with sensible information about Tourette syndrome.

- Explain to them the nature of the tics and the fact that the child has no real control over them.

- Emphasise that the child should be treated as normally as possible and that the relative should not make a big issue out of the tics.

- Invite the relative to a clinic appointment with a specialist who can include the relative in the discussion and answer any questions they might have.

- Above all, try to keep on good terms with relatives, as it is important for children to feel part of a family system. This is particularly important if the child is isolated from peers in and outside of school. Relatives who understand are also useful people to have as child minders.

Parents and their partners

Looking after a child with Tourette syndrome can be extremely exhausting. Children need their parents to be strong and supportive. It is therefore vitally important that parents look after themselves. Some parents, when they learn of their child's diagnosis, feel they cannot enjoy their hobbies or work and give up previous interests. This may be due to guilt, worry about financial costs or simply the feeling that they have to dedicate every ounce of energy into looking after their child. Unless it is absolutely necessary, parents should not give up on hobbies and interests. Tourette syndrome should not dominate parents' lives. If it does then it may leave them mentally drained and exhausted. In order to stay active, fresh and alert:

- Relax – take up yoga, go swimming, go for a walk or take time out to read an interesting novel.

- Keep things in perspective – be aware that many children have all sorts of difficulties and that having a child with Tourette syndrome does not mean that parents have the monopoly on parental stress.

- Talk to others – seek out supportive friends and relatives.

- Talk to other parents in a similar situation – there are many local support groups and charities where parents can contact each other. Seeing others who are in a similar position helps one feel less isolated. Parents may even be able to help other parents by exchanging tips and coping mechanisms.

- If parents have a partner, then it is important to look after each other. Different people will react differently so be sensitive to each other's needs.

- Treat yourself once in a while. This does not have to be expensive: it can be simply making time for a cup of coffee without being disturbed, buying your favourite magazine, taking a walk in the sunshine or visiting friends.

- Book a child minder or ask a relative to look after your children and go out and enjoy yourself with a trip to the cinema or a restaurant.

A relaxed parent is in a better frame of mind to deal with and cope with their child's challenging behaviour. We find that the more the parent is calm and supportive, the more the child is able to cope with the tics.

At home

On the whole, most parents say they can cope with motor tics as long as they are not painful for the child. If the tic is painful then gentle massage of the muscle may help. If the pain persists and is unbearable then it is worth visiting the doctor who may prescribe short-term analgesics. For motor tics that involve the sudden outward movements of limbs it is sensible not to have breakable objects such as vases or ornaments nearby. Be careful also of holding hot cups of tea or coffee near your child. This applies when out in public as well, such as when watching a football match.

Often it is the loud repetitive vocal tics that cause most of the problems at home. These are hard to ignore and can cause a great deal of tension for the whole family. If you want peace and quiet then a set of good old-fashioned earplugs can be a blessing. Watching television together causes a lot of difficulties for siblings. In many cases, the child with vocal tics may be sent to another room to watch television. This is unfortunate as it just adds to the feeling of low self-worth that the child may already have. It takes him away from sharing experiences with those with whom he should feel most comfortable. If watching television together is a really big problem and it is having a major effect on the siblings and the rest of the family and it is too unbearable, then consider purchasing a set of dual- or multi-headed headphones that plug into the television. Thus, at least the child will be able to remain in the same room as his siblings. Anything that reduces stress will be beneficial. That is why the time period immediately after school has finished is usually the most difficult time for parents. Children try to keep their tics controlled as much as possible during school, and when they come home, they discharge their tics like a kettle letting off steam. It is a credit to you and your home if your child does this, as it shows that the one place where he can be himself is home. Be prepared for this 'letting off steam' after school. Let your children run around and tire themselves out.

In public

Many children with tics are so used to their own symptoms that they do not see any particular problem with having tics. As one sibling pointed out to us in clinic, 'It's not my brother's problem, it's the people around him.' Dealing with members of the public and their reaction to your child's tics can cause hurt, embarrassment, anger and sadness. Many parents get tired of explaining or apologising on behalf of their child. Like most things in life, ignorance leads to prejudice. When out in public, remember that most people know very little about Tourette syndrome. Thus, you can choose to ignore stares and accept that people tend to look at things that are different. This is natural: people all stare at other people if they are wearing something unusual, or are very thin, or fat, or from a different race or culture, or even if they have a disability. One way of coping with stares is to train yourself and your child to think that people are staring because they are curious and interested.

Several parents have told us that they still think about comments that were said to their child over ten years ago. It is not the comment that has upset them but the fact that they did not say anything back to the stranger and just accepted it. It is worthwhile having a set of stock phrases for replying to comments and critical stares. In fact, you could see this as an opportunity to educate the public about Tourette syndrome! Say something such as, 'I'm sorry that you seem to be so upset, but my child cannot help coughing out loud. He has a tic disorder known as Tourette syndrome.' If the stranger shows some interest then you can say a bit more. Remember to keep your statement polite. If necessary, be firm but do not shout or get angry. Also note that in this example you are not apologising for your son's tics per se; you are apologising for the fact that the stranger is upset.

You might want to teach your child a similar approach and this is something you could practise with role play. Teaching your child to apologise after any vocal tics that involve offensive words is particularly important. The majority of people do not mind offensive words if there is a genuine apology immediately afterwards.

Some children and adults carry cards with information on Tourette syndrome, which can also be helpful. These cards can be obtained from your child's health professional or local Tourette support group. By remaining calm in public, you are also being a good role model for your child.

18

Dealing with Behavioural Problems

We often get asked about behavioural problems in clinic. In particular, we are often asked whether the behaviour is due to Tourette syndrome or is simply defiant or naughty. It is often difficult to judge. The only answer we have is that 'planned' mischief, that is, behaviour that is premeditated, is not due to Tourette syndrome per se.

We are also asked about coprolalia, which, as we mentioned in the first part of this book, is extremely rare in children. Any rude outbursts that are a result of tics usually occur out of context, that is, not in an argument or as part of an angry exchange or gesture. The child will also be shocked and embarrassed by it and probably apologetic.

Unless a child can verbalise why he or she felt the urge to carry out a particular behaviour, the parents have to make a decision as to whether their child had a degree of control over it or whether it was impulsive. You know your child best so go with your instincts.

All children can be naughty, defiant, aggressive, impulsive and rude. A child with Tourette syndrome and associated behavioural difficulties will show a lot more of the above oppositional behaviour than a typically developing child and will therefore need more help in terms of discipline (rules and standards for acceptable behaviour) and behavioural management (learning appropriate behaviours).

It is also worth noting that the more exhausting and challenging the child is, the more likely that he will receive negative and critical comments from parents and teachers. This may lead to the child developing a poor self-image and be lacking in confidence, and he may start mixing with the wrong crowd and drift into antisocial behaviour. Thus, a parent of a child with Tourette syndrome has to work extra hard to deal with the defiant child, but it will be worth it in the end.

Being prepared

It helps to plan ahead and prevent behavioural problems from starting, or at least have in place effective strategies if they do start. Wherever you go, be prepared to leave early. If your child is going out with other children, then talk to the supervising adult beforehand. Explain that your child may have difficulties and it would be helpful if someone could look out for early signs of excitable behaviour.

If going to the cinema or theatre, choose aisle seats that enable you to make a quick exit if behaviour gets out of hand. If going to a place where you have to wait for a long period of time, such as a restaurant or airport, make sure you have plenty of activities to distract your child. This could include books, drawing materials and, dare we admit it, electronic gadgets such as iPads. Choose restaurants that serve food quickly or have a buffet service. Think about seating arrangements. It may be better to sit in between your children to stop them fighting and causing a scene. Go to shopping malls when they are less crowded and there is less stimulation.

Behavioural management

The basic premise in managing behaviour is that most children want some sort of attention. This is particularly pertinent to those children with Tourette syndrome and associated ADHD. If children do not get positive attention regularly, they will seek out negative attention, whatever that may be, and do their very best to get it. Thus, if possible, ignore attention-seeking behaviour (unless it is dangerous or violent). Remember to focus on the behaviour and not the child. You still love your child but not the behaviour. If limits and boundaries are broken use the strategies mentioned below.

Getting your child to do the things you want him to do

If carrying out a particular behaviour leads to some sort of reward (positive or negative attention) then it is more likely that the child will carry out the same behaviour again. Thus, if there is acceptable behaviour and it is rewarded with praise, the child is likely to continue it. If there is acceptable behaviour and it is not rewarded with praise, then it is likely that the behaviour will diminish. Therefore, if you want good behaviour to continue, you must keep praising and rewarding it in some small way. This can be encouraging words, pats on the back, hugs, or simply saying 'I'm really proud of you.' It is a good idea to vary the praise so the child does not get bored. Keep a close eye on good behaviour and remember to reward it with praise if you want it to continue.

On the other hand, if there is unacceptable behaviour and you reward it with more attention than a simple verbal 'no' – maybe getting annoyed and screaming at your child – then it is likely that the behaviour will continue. If there is unacceptable behaviour and there is no reward then it is likely that the unacceptable behaviour will diminish.

For a younger child (aged five to ten years), star charts and sticker books are helpful. If he accomplishes a task, such as tidying his bedroom every day for a week, he gets a sticker or star each day. If he has enough stickers at the end of the week he gets a small treat or token. The tokens can be built up to purchase something special at the end of the month. This works best if the child has some sort of involvement, such as choosing the treat or negotiating, within reason, how many stickers are needed to get a treat. To avoid this becoming monotonous, apply this to different behaviours as each behaviour improves. You should also vary the stickers and treats.

Praising your child and setting limits

Catch your child being good and praise this behaviour immediately. As discussed above, this will lead to the acceptable behaviour being more likely to re-occur. Be specific about the praise and label the behaviour that you are praising so the child clearly understands. The typical child with Tourette syndrome may need more praise than other children.

Set firm boundaries and limits. The child with Tourette syndrome and ADHD may test your limits and boundaries to the full. When setting limits and giving instructions:

- Be brief but clear.

- Specify the desired behaviour you want.

- Avoid trivial rules and commands. *Don't* have rules about flicking channels on the remote control. *Do* have rules about hitting. Aim to have five or ten rules, not hundreds.

- Agree the house rules with your partner.

- Use 'when–then' commands: *when* you have tidied your bed *then* you can play.

- Praise good behaviour.

- Make sure there are consequences for not following instructions.

- Be consistent.

Believe it or not, deep down inside, children want to get praise and they want to please you! They are therefore more likely to follow instructions that are said in a positive rather than a negative way. For instance, if a child walks on the carpet in muddy shoes and you say, 'Don't walk on the carpet with muddy shoes,' the likelihood is that he will do the same next time. If you were to reframe the request and instead say, 'It would be really good if you took off your muddy shoes before walking on the carpet,' then the child is more likely to respond to this and take off his shoes next time.

If your child is not paying attention then make sure he can see your face. Hold him by the shoulders, look straight into his eyes and be firm with your command. It is okay to look cross, but avoid shouting. If limits are broken then try using time out or 'response cost', as described below.

Time out

Time out should be used rarely and for serious things only, such as fighting, rudeness to you or destructive and violent behaviour. This involves sending or taking your child to another room where he can calm down. Agree on a safe room to calm down in. Don't use the kitchen or garage where there will be sharp implements and tools. His bedroom is okay. Some parents say this does not work since their child just plays with all his things in the bedroom. However, time out is exactly what it says: time out from your attention. Time away from you. This might be you not speaking or listening to him for that period of time. So it should not be thought of as a punishment. Think of it as a positive way to calm down. Unless he is extremely violent, it is important to ignore your child while in time out.

Recent developments by Dan Siegel and Tina Payne Bryson (2012) in applying parenting strategies, emphasise the helpfulness of tuning in to your child's emotional well-being and helping him to solve problems and describe his feelings and thoughts. Dr Siegel's work emphasises the importance of understanding and working with brain development. This understanding underpins the most helpful approach a parent can take when interacting with their child (Seigel and Payne Bryson 2015). The book, TED Talks and general work by the authors is worth reviewing.[2]

Response cost

Response cost relates to the removal of privileges or payment of a fine. Many parents say their children do not seem that bothered by this, but they still persist with this as most children dislike privileges being taken away from them even if they cannot admit to it. To avoid seeming as if you are endlessly penalising your children, counteract this with positive praise for good behaviour.

If your child has done something such as stolen sweets from a shop, make him go to the shop to apologise and pay for them. If he has damaged the neighbour's fence, then he should be made to repair it or at least do chores to pay for it. This way your child will see that he has to be responsible for his actions.

---

2. See www.youtube.com/watch?v=kH-BO1rJXbQ, www.youtube.com/watch?v=LiyaSr5aeho and www.drdansiegel.com/resources/video_clips/#Q29ubmVjdCB3aXRoIEtpZHM=

Figure 18.1 gives guidance on the frequency of use of these various behavioural management strategies.

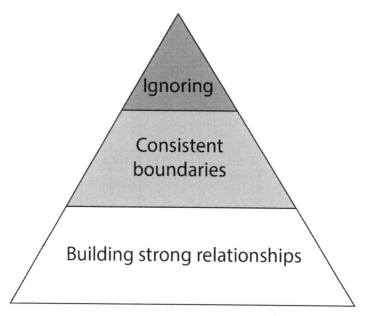

Figure 18.1 Behavioural management strategies

If there are two parents, it is important to provide a united front. Children easily see the difference in opinions and are quick to play one parent off the other.

A final comment

If at all possible, try not to lose your temper and try to stay calm. You are a role model for your child. We tend to lose our temper when things have been building up, when we are not relaxed, when we are tired, hungry and stressed. Therefore, remember to look after yourself and your health. This way, you will be in a better frame of mind when dealing with your child.

19

Improving Your Child's Self-Esteem

'Self-esteem' is a term used to describe how we feel about ourselves most of the time. People with high self-esteem generally feel good about themselves the majority of the time. They are usually confident and outgoing, and are likely to be sociable. People with low self-esteem feel uncertain or negative about themselves the majority of the time. They may not feel as good, clever or attractive as other people. They often feel other people are better than them and as a result they tend to be reluctant to join in or they will withdraw from taking part in activities, including social events.

The development of an individual's self-esteem usually starts in childhood and is built on over many years. Some people may be genetically predisposed to developing a form of low self-esteem, particularly if there is a history of clinical depression in the family. For the majority of people, the message that children feel they are not worthy or not any good usually comes from parents, family members, other children and occasionally teachers. These important people shape a child's view of themselves, as they are the people the child looks up to for guidance and approval.

Tourette syndrome and self-esteem

The strongest predictor of self-esteem seems to relate to how a family communicates. A child with Tourette syndrome may have disruption in family function for one or more of several reasons. He may be criticised by parents, siblings and other members of the family for making noises or fidgeting for a prolonged period of time. If a child is told that he is 'naughty' enough times, he might start believing he really is.

Many children with a severe form of Tourette syndrome that involves loud vocal tics or obvious, painful motor jerks can still feel confident about themselves so long as they have supportive peer groups, parents and teachers. The outlook and prognosis for a child who is well supported is likely to be good since the child will accept who he is and be content with his own ability. He will recognise his own weaknesses and strengths. This will be mainly due to the attitude of his family and peer group, who accept that the 'annoying' loud noises that the child suddenly makes are part of his condition and cannot be helped.

We have seen many children with severe tics in our clinics who have very positive outgoing personalities. It is undoubtedly the positive attitude and support from parents that make the child resilient and thus popular amongst his peers.

There is a range of factors which may affect an individual's self-esteem, which are described in the following pages. The list in Figure 19.1 was compiled by a group of children with Tourette syndrome.

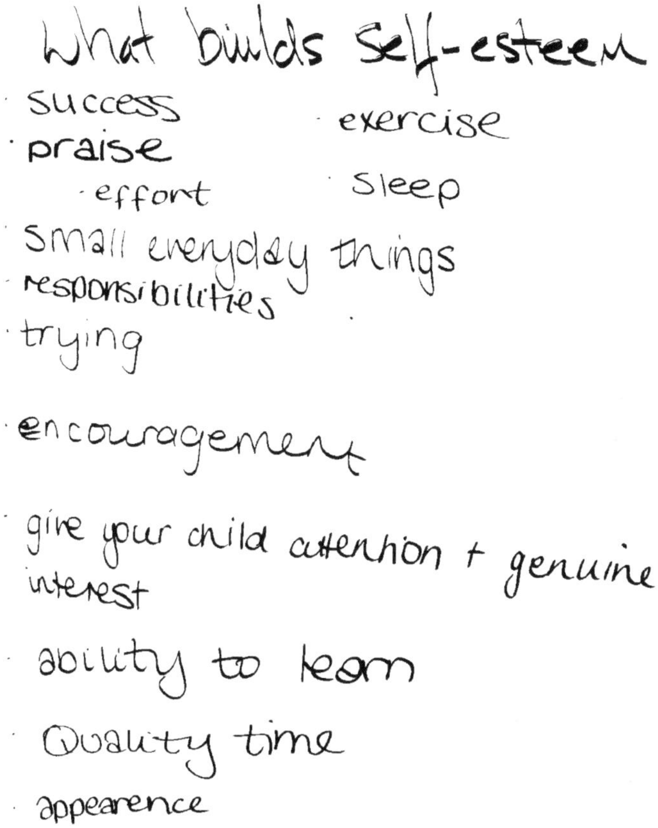

What builds Self-esteem
· success
· praise   · exercise
     · effort   · Sleep
· Small everyday things
· responsibilities
· trying

· encouragement

· give your child attention + genuine
  interest

· ability to learn

· Quality time

· appearence

Figure 19.1 Building self-esteem

Improving self-esteem
Praise

Children need to know that their parents love them and have faith in them regardless of their abilities. All children want to please their parents and get a positive response. It makes them feel secure and confident. As the child develops, he or she looks towards parents for some sort of feedback. This even continues into adulthood. So the message is: praise whenever you can but do so with good sense and limits.

Support and encouragement

In order to get a child to try things, he needs to feel that his parents support him no matter what happens. Parents should give lots of praise when their child achieves something but, equally, when something does not work out, the child needs to know that Mum and Dad do not think any worse of him. Be encouraging with comments like 'Not to worry, you did your best', and 'Well done for giving it a go – I'm proud of you.' Showing faith in your child's ideas and abilities is important for self-belief.

Responsibility at home or school

School is also helpful for building up self-esteem. This can be something simple: being in charge of the pencils and making sure they are sharpened, or choosing what story should be read by the class out of a selection. Having tasks and duties can be important to children with Tourette syndrome as they can feel good about their contribution, and it can also enable them to take breaks from the classroom if they need to tic.

Give them lots of experiences

Give the children the opportunity to experience a variety of things, such as museums, cinemas, theatres, libraries and clubs. Encourage hobbies and leisure activities. Praising children for strengths such as caring for his pets or getting along with his friends is invaluable for self-esteem and encourages your child to feel good about himself. You are not praising an achievement but a character trait.

Teach your child to cope with disappointment

Things don't always go our way so it is important that we learn to cope with disappointment. Help your child cope by acknowledging how he must be feeling when things go wrong. Praise the child for trying. It may be helpful to tell your child how you felt disappointed in a similar situation in your childhood but that something good came out of it in the end.

Plan regular individual play dates

There is good evidence that fairly brief in duration, structured, individual play dates can enhance self-esteem, facilitate friendships and teach children the skills they need for teenage social interactions. The excellent book by Fred Frankel (2010), *Friends Forever: How Parents Can Help Their Kids Make and Keep Good Friends*, is a helpful guide which describes a programme for planning play dates. If your child struggles to communicate with other children then role playing these skills first can be useful. In the play dates, it is important to ensure that plenty of social interaction results from the children's time together and it is recommended that a primary focus on playing computer games is avoided.

Actively listen to your child

Let your child know that you are actually listening to him even when he is arguing or complaining. Repeating things back to clarify what has been said is often a good way of letting children know that you have heard them. It also prevents any misunderstanding. Use non-judgemental questions when your child has done something that may meet with disapproval. For example, avoid saying, 'Why did you do that?' and instead say, 'I wonder what made you do that?' Be sympathetic and reflect his feelings, saying things such as 'That must feel frustrating,' or 'I'm not surprised you feel angry.' Again, this shows that you are listening to your child and he is more likely to respect you for this.

Be generous with love and affection

Show your child you love him by giving old-fashioned hugs and kisses. Tell him directly that you enjoy his company. Let your child see you demonstrating love and affection for key people in your life such as partners and relatives. This allows your child to express affection to others, which will also enhance his own self-esteem in the long term.

Final thoughts

Living with and loving a child with Tourette syndrome and associated challenges is not always easy. Very often, you will need additional skills, patience and, importantly, knowledge to navigate this difficult but potentially also enriching path. It can be helpful if your child can think about tics as 'friends' that they need to live with. Friends come and go, can be annoying sometimes and funny at other times, but they are important to know and understand well. If your son or daughter has a diagnosis of Tourette syndrome it is likely that tics are going to be with him or her for several years, at least until they reach early adulthood. All the time tics will be in the background, a bit like a friend. Building resiliency through managing challenging situations has been remarked on by many youngsters with tics. Often children will report that having to live with tics makes them a more sensitive, reliable and 'tuned in' person. Importantly, having Tourette syndrome is only one aspect of your child and through emphasising their strengths and talents, in addition to supporting their challenges, you can enable them to enjoy family life, friendships, hobbies and school like any other child.

Glossary

Attention deficit hyperactivity disorder
A developmental disorder involving difficulties with attention, impulsivity and hyperactivity.

Autism spectrum disorder
A developmental disorder with symptoms affecting social communication, verbal and non-verbal communication, and the need for routines and rituals.

Candidate gene
Any gene likely to cause a specific disease or disorder.

Coprographia
The urge to write obscene words.

Coprolalia
Repetitive use of socially unacceptable words or phrases.

Copropraxia
Making obscene gestures.

DNA (deoxyribonucleic acid)
A molecule that contains genetic information in living organisms.

Dopamine
A neurotransmitter found in the brain involved with movement.

Dyscalculia
A developmental disorder that affects the skills involved in accurate and fluent word reading and spelling.

Dysgraphia
A developmental disorder affecting writing.

Dyslexia
A developmental disorder that affects the skills involved in accurate and fluent word reading and spelling.

Dyspraxia
A developmental disorder affecting fine and gross motor movement.

Echolalia
Repeating other people's words.

Echopraxia
Imitating other people's gestures or movements.

Executive function
A group of behaviours such as planning, organisation, working memory and motivation.

Exposure with response prevention
A strategy used in behavioural therapy in which the individual experiences a feared behaviour without trying to neutralise it and then allows the fear to reduce spontaneously.

Genetic linkage
The tendency for genes close together to be inherited together.

Habit reversal training
A type of behaviour therapy that empowers clients to control tics.

Habituation
A mechanism in which a response (such as fear) reduces over time by itself.

Intellectual disability
A significant level of impairment with thinking and everyday behaviour which requires additional support and an adapted environment.

Neuroleptic
A classification of medicines, also known as antipsychotics or major tranquillisers.

Neurotransmitter
A chemical carrying nerve impulses across a synapse.

Obsessive compulsive disorder
A disorder involving recurrent, intrusive thoughts known as obsessions, and the need to perform certain habits and routines, known as compulsions.

Paliphenomena
Repetition of one's own words or gestures.

Premonitory urge
A sensation or feeling that immediately precedes a motor or vocal tic.

Presynaptic receptor
A synapse is the gap between nerve endings. Neurotransmitters are transported across this gap. There are two types of receptors at the nerve ending. The presynaptic receptor is the site where neurotransmitters are sent from. The neurotransmitters are then received at the postsynaptic receptors.

Serotonin
A neurotransmitter in the brain involved in mood, anxiety and movement.

Tics
An involuntary, rapid, recurrent, non-rhythmic motor or vocal action.

Titre
A measurement of the amount or concentration of a substance in a solution. It usually refers to the amount of antibodies found in a patient's blood.

Waxing and waning
The naturally occurring increase and decrease in frequency and severity of tics.

References

American Psychiatric Association (2013) *Diagnostic and Statistical Manual of Mental Disorders* (5th edn). Washington, DC: American Psychiatric Association.

Baron-Cohen, S., Mortimore, C., Moriarty, J., Izaquirre, J. and Robertson, M. (1999) 'The prevalence of Gille de la Tourette's syndrome in children and adolescents with autism.' *Journal of Child Psychology and Psychiatry 40*, 2, 213–218.

Blount, T.H., Lockhart, A.L.T., Garcia, R.V., Raj, J.J. and Peterson, A.L. (2014) 'Intensive outpatient comprehensive behavioral intervention for tics: A case series.' *World Journal of Clinical Cases 2*, 10, 569–577.

Boaler, J. (2010) *The Elephant in the Classroom: Helping Children Learn and Love Maths.* London: Souvenir Press Ltd.

Bodeck, S., Lappe, C. and Evers, S. (2015) 'Tic-reducing effects of music in patients with Tourette's syndrome: Self-reported and objective analysis.' *Journal of the Neurological Sciences 352*, 1–2, 41–47.

Braaten, E. and Willoughby, B. (2014) *Bright Kids Who Can't Keep Up: Help Your Child Overcome Slow Processing Speed and Succeed in a Fast-Paced World.* New York: Guilford Press.

Burd, L., Freeman, R.D., Klug, M.G. and Kerbeshian, J. (2005) 'Tourette syndrome and learning disabilities.' *BMC Pediatrics 5*, 34–40.

Burd, L., Li, Q., Kerbeshian, J., Klug, M.G. and Freeman, R.D. (2009) 'Tourette syndrome and co-morbid pervasive developmenatal disorders.' *Journal of Child Neurology 24*, 170–175.

Canitano, R. and Vivanti, G. (2007) 'Tics and Tourette syndrome in autism spectrum disorders.' *Autism 11*, 19–28.

Carlo, J., Piedad, P. and Cavanna, A.E. (2016) 'Depression in Tourette syndrome: A controlled and comparison study.' *Journal of Neurological Sciences 364*, 128–132.

Cath, D.C., Hedderly, T., Ludolph, A., Stern, J.S. *et al.* (ESSTS Guidelines Group) (2011) 'European clinical guidelines for Tourette Syndrome and other tic disorders. Part I: Assessment. *European Child and Adolescent Psychiatry 20*, 4, 155–171.

Cavanna, A.E. and Rickards, H. (2013) 'The psychopathological spectrum of Gilles de la Tourette syndrome.' *Neuroscience & Biobehavioral Reviews 37*, 1008–1015.

Chang, S., Himle, M., Woods, D., Tucker, B. and Piacentini, J. (2009) 'Psychometric properties of a brief parent-report instrument for assessing tic severity in children with chronic tic disorders.' *Child & Family Behavior Therapy 31*, 3, 181–191.

Christie, D. and Jassi, A. (2002) "'Oh no he doesn't!", "Oh yes he does!":
Comparing parent and teacher perceptions in Tourette's syndrome.' *Clinical Child Psychology and Psychiatry 7*, 553–558.

Crawford, F.C., Ait-Ghezala, G., Morris, M., Sutcliffe, M.J. *et al.* (2003) 'Translocation breakpoint in two unrelated Tourette syndrome cases, within a region previously linked to the disorder.' *Human Genetics 113*, 154–161.

Dale, R. and Heyman, I. (2002) 'Post-streptococcal autoimmune psychiatric and movement disorders in children.' *British Journal of Psychiatry 181*, 3, 188–190.

Derisley, J., Heyman, I., Robinson, S. and Turner, C. (2008) *Breaking Free from OCD: A CBT Guide for Young People and Their Families.* London: Jessica Kingsley Publishers.

Diniz, J.B., Rosario-Campos, M.C., Hounie, A.G, Curi, M. *et al.* (2006) 'Chronic tics and Tourette syndrome in patients with obsessive compulsive disorder.' *Journal of Psychiatric Research 40*, 487–493.

Evans, D.W., Leckman, J.F., Carter, A., Reznick, J.S. *et al.* (1997) 'Ritual, habit, and perfectionism: The prevalence and development of compulsive-like behavior in normal young children.' *Child Development 68*, 58–68.

Felling, R.J. and Singer, H.S. (2011) 'Neurobiology of Tourette syndrome: Current status and need for further investigation. *Journal of Neuroscience 31*, 35, 12387–12395.

Frankel, F. (2010) *Friends Forever: How Parents Can Help Their Kids Make and Keep Good Friends.* San Francisco, CA: Jossey-Bass.

Freeman, R.D., Fast, D., Burd, L., Kerbeshian, J., Robertson, M.M. and Sandor, P. (2000) 'An international perspective on Tourette syndrome: Selected findings from 3,500 individuals in 22 countries.' *Developmental Medicine & Child Neurology 42*, 436–447.

Gadow, K.D., Sverd, J., Sprafkin, J., Nolan, E.E. and Grossman, S. (1999) 'Long-term methylphenidate therapy in children with comorbid attention-deficit hyperactivity disorder and chronic multiple tic disorder.' *Archives of General Psychiatry 56*, 330–336.

Geller, D.A., Biederman, J., Stewart, S.E., Mullin, B. *et al.* (2003) 'Which SSRI? A meta-analysis of pharmacotherapy trials in pediatric obsessive-compulsive disorder.' *American Journal of Psychiatry 160*, 1919–1928.

Giedd, J.N., Rapoport, J.L., Garvey, M.A., Perlmutter, S. and Swedo, S.E. (2000) 'MRI assessment of children with obsessive-compulsive disorder or tics associated with streptococcal infection.' *American Journal of Psychiatry 157*, 2, 281–283.

Harris, K., Graham, S., Mason, L. and Friedlander, B. (2010) *Powerful Writing Strategies for All Students. Reciprocal Teaching at Work: Powerful Strategies and Lessons for Improving Reading Comprehension International Literacy Association* (2nd rev. edn). London: EDS Publications Ltd.

Hassler, R. and Dieckmann, G. (1973) 'Relief of OCD, Phobias and Tics by Stereotactic Coagulations of the Rostral Intralaminar and Medial-Thalamic Nuclei.' In L.V. Laitinen and K.E. Livingston (eds) *Surgical Approaches in Psychiatry. Proceedings of the Third International Congress of Psychosurgery*, 206–212. Cambridge: Garden City Press.

Heyman, I. (1997) 'Children with obsessive compulsive disorder.' *British Medical Journal 315*, 444.

Heyman, I., Matrix-Cols, D. and Fineberg, N.A. (2006) 'Obsessive-compulsive disorder.' *British Medical Journal 333*, 424–429.

Himle, M.B., Freitag, M., Walther, M., Franklin, S.A., Ely, L. and Woods, D.W. (2012) 'A randomized pilot trial comparing videoconference versus face-to-face delivery of behavior therapy for childhood tic disorders.' *Behaviour Research and Therapy 50*, 9, 565–570.

Ho, C.S., Chen, H.J., Chiu, N.C., Shen, E.Y. and Lue, H.C. (2009) 'Short term sulpiride treatment of children and adolescents with Tourette syndrome or chronic tic disorder.' *Journal of the Formosan Medical Association 108*, 788–793.

Hounie, A.G., do Rosario-Campos, M.C., Diniz, J.B., Shavitt, R.G. *et al.* (2006) 'Obsessive-compulsive disorder in Tourette syndrome.' *Advances in Neurology 99*, 22–38.

Huckeba, W., Chapieski, L., Hiscock, M. and Glaze, D. (2008) 'Arithmetic performance in children with Tourette syndrome: Relative contribution of cognitive and attentional factors.' *Journal of Clinical and Experimental Neuropsychology 30*, 4, 410–420.

Hudziak, J.J., van Beijsterveldt, C.E.M., Althoff, R.R., Stanger, C. *et al.* (2004) 'Genetic and environmental contributions to the child behaviour checklist obsessive compulsive scale.' *Archives of General Psychiatry 61*, 608–616.

Hyde, T.M., Aaronson, B.A., Randolph, C., Rickler, K.C. and Weinberger, D.R. (1992) 'Relationship of birth weight to the phenotypic expression of Gilles de la Tourette's syndrome in monozygotic twins.' *Neurology 42*, 652–658.

Jackson, G.M., Mueller, S.C., Hambleton, K. and Hollis, C.P. (2007) 'Enhanced cognitive control in Tourette Syndrome during task uncertainty.' *Experimental Brain Research 182*, 3, 357–364.

Jackson, G.M., Draper, A., Dyke, K., Pépés, S.E. and Jackson, S.R. (2015) 'Inhibition, disinhibition, and the control of action in Tourette syndrome.' *Trends in Cognitive Science 19*, 11, 655–665.

Jensen, C.M. and Steinhausen, H.C. (2015) 'Comorbid mental disorders in children and adolescents with attention-deficit/hyperactivity disorder in a large nationwide study.' *ADHD Attention Deficit Hyperactivity Disorder 7*, 1, 27–38.

Jones, K., Daley, D., Hutchings, J., Bywater, T. and Eames, C. (2008) 'Efficacy of the Incredible Years Programme as an early intervention for children with conduct problems and ADHD: Long-term follow-up.' *Child: Care, Health and Development 34*, 380–390.

Jonnal, A.H., Gardner, C.O., Prescott, C.A. and Kendler, K.S. (2000) 'Obsessive and compulsive symptoms in a general population sample of female twins.' *American Journal of Medical Genetics (Neuropsychiatric Genetics) 96*, 791–796.

Kadesjo, B. and Gillberg, C. (2000) 'Tourette's disorder: Epidemiology and co-morbidity in primary school children.' *Journal of the American Academy of Child and Adolescent Psychiatry 39*, 548–555.

Kenney, C.J., Hunter, C.B., Mejia, N.I. and Jankovic, J. (2007) 'Tetrabenazine in the treatment of Tourette syndrome.' *Journal of Pediatric Neurology 5*, 9–13.

Khalifa, N. and von Knorring, A.L. (2005) 'Tourette syndrome and other tic disorders in a total population of children: Clinical assessment and background.' *Acta Paediatrica 94*, 11, 1608–1614.

Kostanecka-Endress, T., Banaschewski, T., Kinkelbur, J., Wullner, I. *et al.* (2003). 'Disturbed sleep in children with Tourette syndrome: A polysomnographic study.' *Journal of Psychosomatic Research 55*, 23–29.

Kroisel, P.M., Petek, E., Emberger, W., Windpassinger, W., Wladika, W. and Wagner, K. (2001) 'Candidate region for Gilled e la Tourette syndrome at 7q31.' *American Journal of Medical Genetics 101*, 259–261.

Kurlan, R., Lichter, D. and Hewitt, D. (1989) 'Sensory tics in Tourette's syndrome.' *Neurology 39*, 5, 731–734.

Leckman, J.F. (2002) 'Tourette's syndrome.' *Lancet 360*, 1577–1586.

Leckman, J.F., Hardin, M.T., Riddle, M.A., Stevenson, J., Ort, S.I. and Cohen, D.J. (1991) 'Clonidine treatment of Gilles de la Tourette's syndrome.' *Archives of General Psychiatry 48*, 324–328.

Leckman, J.F., Grice, D.E., Boardman, J., Zhang, H. *et al.* (1997) 'Symptoms of obsessive compulsive disorder.' *American Journal of Psychiatry 154*, 7, 911–917.

Leckman, J.F., Riddle, M.A., Hardin, M.T., Ort, S.I. *et al.* (1989) 'The Yale Global Tic Severity Scale: Initial testing of a clinician-rated scale of tic severity.' *Journal of the American Academy of Child & Adolescent Psychiatry 28*, 4, 566–573.

Lewin, A.B., Storch, E.A., Conelea, C.A., Woods, D.W. *et al.* (2011) 'The roles of anxiety and depression in connecting tic severity and functional impairment.' *Journal of Anxiety Disorders 25*, 164–168.

Liu, W.Y., Wang, H.S., Hsu, L.Y., Wong, A.M., Chen, C.L. and Lien, H.Y. (2011) 'Health-related physical fitness management for a child with Tourette syndrome.' *Chang Gung Medical Journal 34*, 6 (Suppl.), 4–9.

Maciunas, R.J., Maddux, B.N., Riley, D.E., Whitney, C.M. *et al.* (2007) 'Prospective randomized double-blind trial of bilateral thalamic deep brain stimulation in adults with Tourette syndrome.' *Journal of Neurosurgery 107*, 1004–1014.

Mathews, C.A., Waller, J., Glidden, D., Lowe, T.L. *et al.* (2004) 'Self injurious behaviour in Tourette syndrome: Correlates with impulsivity and impulse control.' *Journal of Neurology, Neurosurgery and Psychiatry 75*, 1149–1155.

Matsuda, N., Kono, T., Nonaka, M., Fujio, M. and Kano, Y. (2016) 'Self-initiated coping with Tourette's syndrome: Effect of tic suppression on QOL.' *Brain and Development 38*, 2, 233–241.

McGuire J.F., Arnold, E., Park, J.M., Nadeau, J.M. *et al.* (2015) 'Living with tics: Reduced impairment and improved quality of life for youth with chronic tic disorders.' *Psychiatry Research 225*, 571–579.

McKinlay, D. (2015) *Nix Your Tics! Eliminating Unwanted Tic Symptoms: A How-to Guide for Young People (2nd edn)*. Ontario: Life's A Twitch! Publishing.

Micali, N., Heyman, I., Peter, M., Holton, K. *et al.* (2010) 'Long-term outcomes of obsessive-compulsive disorder: Follow-up of 142 children and adolescents.' *British Journal of Psychiatry 197*, 2, 128–134.

Mink, J.W., Walkup, J., Frey, K.A., Como, P. *et al.* (2006) 'Patient selection and assessment recommendations for deep brain stimulation in Tourette syndrome.' *Movement Disorders 21*, 11, 1831–1838.

Moody, S. (2004) *Dyslexia: A Teenager's Guide*. London: Random House.

Mukaddes, N.M. and Abali, O. (2003) 'Quetiapine treatment of children and adolescents with Tourette's disorder.' *Journal of Child and Adolescent Psychopharmacology 13*, 295–299.

Müller-Vahl, K.R., Buddensiek, N., Geomelas, M. and Emrich, M. (2008) 'The influence of different food and drink on tics in Tourette syndrome.' *Acta Paediatrica 97*, 4, 442–446.

Müller-Vahl, K.R., Cath, D.C., Cavanna, A.E., Dehning, S. *et al.* (ESSTS Guidelines Group) (2011) 'European clinical guidelines for Tourette syndrome and other tic disorders. Part IV: Deep brain stimulation.' *European Child and Adolescent Psychiatry 20*, 4, 209–217.

National Institute for Health and Clinical Excellence (NICE) (2005) *Obsessive-Compulsive Disorder and Body Dysmorphic Disorder: Treatment (NICE Guidelines CG31). Available at www.nice.org.uk/Guidance/CG31, accessed on 29 May 2016.*

National Institute for Health and Clinical Excellence (NICE) (2016) *Attention Deficit Hyperactivity Disorder: Diagnosis and Management (NICE Guidelines CG72). Available at www.nice.org.uk/guidance/cg72, accessed on 29 May 2016.*

Nixon, E., Glazebrook, C., Hollis, C. and Jackson, G.M. (2014) 'Reduced tic symptomatology in Tourette syndrome after an acute bout of exercise an observational study.' *Behavior Modification 38*, 2, 235–263.

Nussey, C., Pistrang, N. and Murphy, T. (2013) 'How does psychoeducation help? A review of the effects of providing information about Tourette syndrome and attention-deficit/hyperactivity disorder.' *Child: Care, Health and Development 39*, 617–627.

Nussey, C., Pistrang, N. and Murphy, T. (2014) 'Does it help to talk about tics? An evaluation of a classroom presentation about Tourette syndrome.' *Child and Adolescent Mental Health 19*, 1, 31–38.

Packer, L.E. and Pruitt, S.K. (2010) *Challenging Kids, Challenged Teachers: Teaching Students with Tourette's, Bipolar Disorder, Executive Dysfunction, OCD, ADHD, and More.* Bethesda, MD: Woodbine House.

Packer-Hopke, L. and Motta, R.W. (2014) 'A preliminary investigation of the effects of aerobic exercise on childhood Tourette's syndrome and OCD.' *Behavior Therapist 37*, 7, 188–192.

Pappert, E.J., Goetz, C.G., Louis, E.D., Blasucci, R.N. and Leurgans, S. (2003) 'Objective assessments of longitudinal outcome in Gilles de la Tourette's syndrome.' *Neurology 61*, 7, 936–940.

Pediatric OCD Treatment Study (POTS) Team (2004) 'Cognitive-behavior therapy, sertraline, and their combination for children and adolescents with obsessive-compulsive disorder: The Pediatric OCD Treatment Study (POTS) randomized controlled trial.' *JAMA 292*, 16, 1969–1976.

Peterson, B.S., Leckman, J.F., Scahill, L., Naftolin, F. *et al.* (1992) 'Hypothesis: Steroid hormones and sexual dimorphisms modulate symptom expression in Tourette's syndrome.' *Psychoneuroendolocrinology 17*, 553–563.

Peterson, B.S., Staib, L., Scahill, L., Zhang, H. *et al.* (2001) 'Regional brain and ventricular volumes in Tourette syndrome.' *Archives of General Psychiatry 58*, 427–440.

Peterson, B.S., Skudlarski, P., Anderseon, A.W., Zhang, H. *et al.* (1998) 'A functional magnetic resonance imaging study of tic suppression in Tourette syndrome.' *Archives of General Psychiatry 55*, 326–333.

Plessen, K.J., Grüner, R., Lundervold, A., Hirsch, J.G. *et al.* (2006) 'Reduced white matter connectivity in the corpus callosum of children with Tourette syndrome.' *Journal of Child Psychology and Psychiatry 47*, 1013–1022.

Porta, M., Maggioni, G., Ottaviani, F. and Schindler, A. (2004) 'Treatment of phonic tics in patients with Tourette's syndrome using botulinum toxin type A.' *Neurological Sciences 24*, 420–423.

Price, R.A., Kidd, K.K., Cohen, D.J., Pauls, D.L. and Leckman, J.F. (1985) 'A twin study of Tourette syndrome.' *Archives of General Psychiatry 42*, 815–820.

Pringsheim, T., Doja, A., Gorman, D., McKinlay, D. *et al.* (2012) 'Canadian guidelines for the evidence-based treatment of tic disorders: Pharmacotherapy.' *Canadian Journal of Psychiatry 57*, 3, 133–143.

Ricketts, E.J., Gilbert, D.L., Zinner, S.H., Mink, J.W. *et al.* (2015a) 'Pilot testing behavior therapy for chronic tic disorders in neurology and developmental pediatrics clinics.' *Journal of Child Neurology 31*, 4, 444–450.

Ricketts, E.J., Goetz, A.R., Capriotti, M.R., Bauer, C.C. *et al.* (2015b) 'A randomized waitlist-controlled pilot trial of voice over internet protocol-delivered behavior therapy for youth with chronic tic disorders.' *Journal of Telemedicine and Telecare 22*, 3, 153–162.

Robertson, M.M. (2006) 'Mood disorders and Gilles de la Tourette's syndrome: An update on prevalence, etiology, comorbidity, clinical associations, and implications.' *Journal of Psychosometric Research 61*, 349–358.

Robertson, M.M. (2015) 'A personal 35 year perspective on Gilles de la Tourette syndrome: Prevalence, phenomenology, comorbidities, and co-existing psychopathologies.' *Lancet Psychiatry 2*, 1, 68–87.

Robertson, M.M., Schnieden, V. and Lees, A.J. (1990) 'Management of Gilles de la Tourette syndrome using sulpiride.' *Clinical Neuropharmacology 13*, 229–235.

Roessner, V., Plessen, K.J., Rothenberger, A., Ludolph, A.G. *et al.* (2011) 'European clinical guidelines for Tourette syndrome and other tic disorders. Part II: Pharmacological treatment. *European Child and Adolescent Psychiatry 20*, 173–196.

Rosenberg, D.R. and Hanna, G.L. (2000) 'Genetic and Imaging strategies in obsessive-compulsive disorder: Potential implications for treatment development.' *Biological Psychiatry 48*, 1210–1222.

Rowe, J., Yuen, H.K. and Dure, L.S. (2013) 'Comprehensive behavioral intervention to improve occupational performance in children with Tourette disorder.' *American Journal of Occupational Therapy 67*, 2, 194–200.

Sacconai, L., Fabiana, V., Manuela, B. and Giambattista, R. (2005) 'Tourette sundrome and chronic tics in a sample of children and adolescents.' *Brain and Development 27*, 349–352.

Sallee, F.R., Nesbitt, L., Jackson, C., Sine, L. and Sethuraman, G. (1997) 'Relative efficacy of haloperidol and pimozide in children and adolescents with Tourette's disorder.' *American Journal of Psychiatry 154*, 1057–1062.

Sanders , M.R., Mazzucchelli, T.G. and Studman, L.J. (2004) 'Stepping Stones Triple P: The theoretical basis and development of an evidence-based positive parenting program for families with a child who has a disability.' *Journal of Intellectual and Developmental Disability 29*, 3, 265–283.

Scahill, L., Chappell, P.B., Kim, Y.S., Schultz, R.T. *et al.* (2001) 'A placebo-controlled study of guanfacine in the treatment of children with tic disorders and attention deficit hyperactivity disorder.' *American Journal of Psychiatry 158*, 1067–1074.

Scahill, L., Leckman, J.F., Schultz, R.T., Katsovich, L. and Peterson, B.S. (2003) 'A placebo-controlled trial of risperidone in Tourette syndrome.' *Neurology 60*, 7, 1130–1135.

Scharf, J.M., Miller, L.L., Mathews, C.A. and Ben-Shlomo, Y. (2012) 'Prevalence of Tourette syndrome and chronic tics in the population-based Avon longitudinal study of parents and children cohort.' *Journal of the American Academy of Child and Adolescent Psychiatry 51*, 2, 192–201.

Servello, D., Porta, M., Sassi, M., Brambilla, A. and Robertson, M.M. (2008). 'Deep brain stimulation in 18 patients with severe Gilles de la Tourette syndrome refractory to treatment: The surgery and stimulation.' *Journal of Neurology Neurosurgery and Psychiatry 79*, 2, 136–142.

Shapiro, E., Shapiro, A.K., Fulop, G., Hubbard, M. *et al.* (1989) 'Controlled study of haloperidol, pimozide and placebo for the treatment of Gilles de la Tourette's syndrome.' *Archives of General Psychiatry 46*, 8, 722–730.

Shaw, P., Greensted, D., Lench, J., Clare, L. *et al.* (2006) 'Intellectual ability and cortical development in children and adolescents.' *Nature 440*, 7084, 676–679.

Siegel, D.J. and Payne Bryson, T. (2012) *The Whole-Brain Child: 12 Proven Strategies to Nurture Your Child's Developing Mind.* London: Robinson.

Siegel, D.J. and Payne Bryson, T. (2015) *No-Drama Discipline: The Whole-Brain Way to Calm the Chaos and Nurture Your Child's Developing Mind.* London: Scribe Publications.

Silver, A.A., Shytle, R.D., Philipp, M.K. and Sanberg, P.R. (1996) 'Case study: Long term potentiation of neuroleptics with transdermal nicotine in Tourette's syndrome.' *Journal of the American Academy of Child and Adolescent Psychiatry 35*, 12, 1631–1636.

Simonic, I., Nyholt, D.R., Gericke, G.S., Gordon, D. *et al.* (2001) 'Further evidence for linkage of Gilles de la Tourette syndrome susceptibility loci on chromosomes 2p11, 8q22 and 11q23-24 in South African Afrikaners.' *American Journal of Medical Genetics 105*, 2, 163–167.

Singer, H.S., Gilbert, D.L., Wolf, D.S., Mink, J.W. and Kurlan, R. (2012) 'Moving from PANDAS to CANS.' *Journal of Pediatrics 160*, 5, 725–731.

Skoog, G. and Skoog, I. (1999) 'A 40-year follow-up of patients with obsessive-compulsive disorder.' *Archives of General Psychiatry 56*, 2, 121–127.

Specht, M.W., Woods, D.W., Piacentini, J., Scahill, L. *et al.* (2011) 'Clinical characteristics of children and adolescents with a primary tic disorder.' *Journal of Developmental and Physical Disabilities 23*, 1, 15–31.

Spencer, T.J., Biederman, J., Faraone, S., Mick, E. *et al.* (2001) 'Impact of tic disorders on ADHD outcome across the life cycle: Findings from a large group of adults with and without ADHD.' *American Journal of Psychiatry 158*, 4, 611–617.

Stewart, S.E., Geller, D.A., Jenike, M., Pauls, D. *et al.* (2004) 'Long-term outcome of pediatric obsessive compulsive disorder: A meta-analysis and qualitative review of the literature.' *Acta Psychiatrica Scandinavica 110*, 1, 4–13.

Storch, E.A., Milsom, V., Lack, C.W., Pence, S.L. Jr, *et al.* (2009) 'Sleep-related problems in youth with Tourette's syndrome and chronic tic disorder.' *Child and Adolescent Mentel Health 14*, 2, 97–103.

Sukhodolsky, D.G., Smith, S.D., McCartney, S.A., Karim, I. and Piasecka, J.B. (2016) 'Behavioral interventions for anger, irritability, and aggression in children and adolescents.' *Journal of Child and Adolescent Psychopharmacology 26*, 1, 58–64.

Swedo, S.E., Leckman, J.F. and Rose, N.R. (2012) 'From research sub group to clinical syndrome: Modifying the PANDAS criteria to describe PANS.' *Pediatrics & Therapeutics 12*, 2, 2.

Swedo, S.E., Leonard, H.L., Garvey, M., Mittleman, D. *et al.* (1998) 'Pediatric autoimmune neuropsychiatric disorders associated with streptococcal infections: Clinical description of the first 50 cases.' *American Journal of Psychiatry 155*, 2, 265–271.

Thompson, M.J.J., Laver-Bradbury, C., Ayres, M., Poidevin, E. *et al.* (2009) 'A small-scale randomized controlled trial of the revised New Forest Parenting Programme for preschoolers with attention deficit hyperactivity disorder.' *European Child and Adolescent Psychiatry 18*, 10, 605–616.

Tourette Syndrome Association International Consortium for Genetics (1999) 'A complete genome screen in sib-pairs affected with Gilles de la Tourette syndrome.' *American Journal of Human Genetics 65*, 1428–1436.

Tourette Syndrome Study Group (2002) 'Treatment of ADHD in children with tics: A randomized controlled trial.' *Neurology 58*, 527–536.

Vandewalle, V., van der Linden, C., Groenewegen, H.J. and Caemaert, J. (1999) 'Stereotactic treatment of Gilles de la Tourette syndrome by high frequency stimulation of thalamus.' *Lancet 353*, 9154, 724.

Vasconcelos, M.S., Sampaio, A.S., Hounie, A.G., Akkerman, F. *et al.* (2007) 'Prenatal, perinatal, and postnatal risk factors in obsessive-compulsive disorder.' *Biological Psychiatry 61*, 301–307.

Verkerk, A.J., Mathews, C.A., Joosse, M., Eussen, B.H., Heutink, P. and Oostra, B.A. (2003) 'CNTNAP2 is disrupted in a family with Gille de la Tourette syndrome and obsessive compulsive disorder.' *Genomics 82*, 1, 1–9.

Visser-Vandewalle, V., Ackermans, L., van der Linden, C., Temel, Y., Tijssen, M.A. *et al.* (2006) 'Deep brain stimulation in Gilles de la Tourette's syndrome.' *Neurosurgery 58*, 3, E590.

Visser-Vandewalle, V., Temel, Y., Boon, P., Vreeling, F. *et al.* (2003) 'Chronic bilateral thalamic stimulation: A new therapeutic approach in intractable Tourette syndrome. Report of three cases.' *Journal of Neurosurgery 99*, 6, 1094–1100.

Wechsler, D. (2014) *Wechsler Intelligence Scale for Children – Fifth Edition.* Bloomington, MN: Pearson.

Woods, D.W., Conelea, C.A. and Himle, M.B. (2010) 'Behavior therapy for Tourette's disorder: Utilization in a community sample and an emerging area of practice for psychologists.' *Professional Psychology Research and Practice 41*, 6, 518–527.

Woods, D.W. and Twohig, M.P. (2008) *Trichotillomania: An ACT-enhanced Behavior Therapy Approach Therapist Guide (Treatments that Work).* New York: Oxford University Press.

Worbe, Y., Mallet, L., Golmard, J.L., Béhar, C. *et al.* (2010) 'Repetitive behaviours in patients with Gilles de la Tourette syndrome: Tics, compulsions, or both?' *PLoS One5*, 9, e12959.

Wright, A., Rickards, H. and Cavanna, A.E. (2012) 'Impulse-control disorders in Gilles de la Tourette syndrome.' *Journal of Neuropsychiatry and Clinical Neurosciences 24*, 16–27.

Yates, R., Edwards, K., King, J., Luzon, O. *et al.* (2016) 'Habit reversal training and educational group treatments for children with tourette syndrome: A preliminary randomised controlled trial.' *Behaviour Research and Therapy 80*, 43–50.

Yoo, H.K., Kim, J.Y. and Kim, C.Y. (2006) 'A pilot study of aripiprazole in children and adolescents with Tourette's disorder.' *Journal of Child and Adolescent Psychopharmacology 16*, 505–506.

Useful Resources and Websites

ADHD

Gantos, J. (2015) *The Key That Swallowed Joey Pigza*. New York: Square Fish.

Horstmann, K. and Steer, J. (2009) *Helping Kids and Teens with ADHD in School: A Workbook for Classroom Support and Managing Transitions*. London: Jessica Kingsley Publishers.

Laver-Bradbury. C.J. (2010) *Step by Step Help for Children with ADHD: A Self-Help Manual for Parents*. London: Jessica Kingsley Publishers.

Rotz, R.D. and Wright, S. (2005) *Fidget to Focus: Outwit Your Boredom. Sensory Strategies for Living with AD*. Bloomington, IN: iUniverse Books.

Yarney, S. and Martin, C. (2013) *Can I tell you about ADHD?: A Guide for Friends, Family and Professionals*. London: Jessica Kingsley Publishers.

Anger, anxiety and OCD

Biegel, G.M. (2009) *Stress Reduction Workbook for Teens: Mindfulness Skills to Help You Deal with Stress* (Teen Instant Help). Oakland, CA: New Harbinger.

Cartwright-Hatton, S. (2007) *Coping with an Anxious or Depressed Child: A Guide for Parents and Carers*. London: Oneworld Publications.

Creswell, C. and Willetts, L. (2013) *Overcoming Your Child's Fears and Worries: A Self-help Guide Using Cognitive Behavioral Techniques*. London: Robinson.

Derisley, J., Heyman, I., Robinson, S. and Turner, C. (2008) *Breaking Free from OCD: A CBT Guide for Young People and Their Families*. London: Jessica Kingsley Publishers.

Ironside, V. (2012) *The Huge Bag of Worries*. London: Hachette.

Jassi, A. (2013) *Can I tell you about OCD?: A Guide for Friends, Family and Professionals*. London: Jessica Kingsley Publishers.

Pudney, W. and Whitehouse, É. (1996) *A Volcano in My Tummy: Helping Children to Handle Anger. A Resource Book for Parents, Caregivers and Teachers*. Gabriola, BC: New Society Publishers.

Wells, J. and Heyman, I. (2006) *Touch and Go Joe: An Adolescent's Experiences of OCD*. London: Jessica Kingsley Publishers.

ASD, friendships and social skills

Attwood, T. (2006) *The Complete Guide to Asperger's Syndrome*. London: Jessica Kingsley Publishers.

Attwood, T. and Grandin, T. (2006) *Asperger's and Girls: World-Renowned Experts Join Those with Asperger's Syndrome to Resolve Issues That Girls and Women Face Every Day!* Arlington, TX: Future Horizons, Inc.

Chidekel, D. (2007) *Parents in Charge: Setting Healthy, Loving Boundaries for You and Your Child*. London: Little, Brown and Co.

Elder, J. and Thomas, M. (2005) *Different Like Me: My Book of Autism Heroes*. London: Jessica Kingsley Publishers.

Frankel, F. (2010) *Friends Forever: How Parents Can Help Their Kids Make and Keep Good Friends*. San Francisco, CA: Jossey-Bass.

Garcia Winner, M. and Crooke. P. (2011) *Socially Curious and Curiously Social*. Great Barrington, MA: North River Press.

Gray, C. (2010) *The New Social Story Book*. Arlington, TX: Future Horizons.

Plummer, D.M. (2012) *Focusing and Calming Games for Children: Mindfulness Strategies and Activities to Help Children to Relax, Concentrate and Take Control*. London: Jessica Kingsley Publishers.

Siegel, D.J. (2014) *Brainstorm: The Power and Purpose of the Teenage Brain*. New York: Scribe Publications.

Siegel, D.J. and Payne Bryson, T. (2012) *The Whole-Brain Child: 12 Proven Strategies to Nurture Your Child's Developing Mind*. London: Robinson.

Executive functioning

Brateen, E. and Willoughby, B. (2014) *Bright Kids Who Can't Keep Up: Help Your Child Overcome Slow Processing Speed and Succeed in a Fast-Paced World*. New York: Guilford Press.

Cooper-Kahn, J. and Dietzel, L.C. (2008) *Late, Lost and Unprepared: A Parents' Guide to Helping Children with Executive Functioning*. Bethesda, MD: Woodbine House.

Guare, R., Dawson, P. and Guare, C. (2012) *Smart But Scattered Teens: The Executive Skills Program for Helping Teens Reach Their Potential*. New York: Guilford Press.

Learning challenges

Boaler, J. (2010) *The Elephant in the Classroom: Helping Children Learn and Love Maths*. London: Souvenir Press Ltd.

Beck, I.L., McKeown, M.G. and Kucan, L. (2013) *Bringing Words to Life: Robust Vocabulary Instruction*. New York: Guilford Press.

Blakemore, S.J. and Frith, U. (2005) *The Learning Brain: Lessons for Education*. Oxford: Blackwell Publishing.

Boon, M. (2014) *Can I tell you about Dyspraxia?: A Guide for Friends, Family and Professionals*. London: Jessica Kingsley Publishers.

Gathercole, S. and Alloway, T.P. (2008) *Working Memory and Learning: A Practical Guide for Teachers*. London: Sage.

Harris, K., Graham, S., Mason, L. and Friedlander, B. (2008) *Powerful Writing Strategies for All Students. Reciprocal Teaching at Work: Powerful Strategies and Lessons for Improving Reading Comprehension International Literacy Association* (2nd rev. edn). Baltimore, MD: Brookes Publishers.

Hultquist, A.M. (2013) *Can I tell you about Dyslexia?: A Guide for Friends, Family And Professionals*. London: Jessica Kingsley Publishers.

Likierman, H. and Muter, V. (2008) *Dyslexia: A Parents' Guide to Dyslexia, Dyspraxia and Other Learning Difficulties*. London: Vermilion.

Moody, S. (2004) *Dyslexia: A Teenager's Guide*. London: Random House.

Tourette syndrome

Buehrens, A. (1990) *Hi, I'm Adam: A Child's Story of Tourette Syndrome.* Duarte, CA: Hope Press.

Buffolano, S. (2008) *Coping with Tourette Syndrome Syndrome: A Workbook for Kids with Tic Disorders.* Oakland, CA: New Harbinger.

Chowdhury, U., Robertson, M., Whallett, L. and Howard, T. (2006) *Why Do You Do That?: A Book about Tourette Syndrome for Children and Young People.* London: Jessica Kingsley Publishers.

Leicester, M. (2013) *Can I tell you about Tourette Syndrome?: A Guide for Friends, Family and Professionals.* London: Jessica Kingsley Publishers.

McKinlay, D. (2015) *Nix Your Tics! Eliminating Unwanted Tic Symptoms: A How-to Guide for Young People (2nd edn).* Ontario: Life's A Twitch! Publishing.

Packer, L.E. and Pruitt, S.K. (2010) *Challenging Kids, Challenged Teachers: Teaching Students With Tourette's, Bipolar Disorder, Executive Dysfunction, OCD, ADHD, and More.* Bethesda, MD: Woodbine House.

Robertson, M.M. and Baron-Cohen, S. (1998) *Tourette Syndrome: The Facts (2nd edn).* Oxford University Press.

Thom, J. (2012) *Welcome to Biscuit Land: A Year in the Life of Touretteshero.* London: Souvenir Press.

Verdellen, C., van de Griendt, J., Kriens, S. and van Oostrum, I. (2011) *Tics: Therapist Manual.* Amsterdam: Boom Publishers.

Woods. D., Piacentini, J., Chang, S.W., Deckersbach, T. *et al.* (2008) *Managing Tourette Syndrome: A Behavioral Intervention for Children and Adults. Therapist Guide (Treatments That Work).* Oxford University Press.

Websites

Tourettes Action

Supports people with Tourette syndrome and those who work with them, and funds research into treatment and diagnosis.

www.tourettes-action.org.uk

Tourette Association of America

Aims to make life better for anyone affected by Tourette and tic disorders, and funds research into the condition.

http://tourette.org

Tourette Canada

Raises awareness and understanding of Tourette syndrome through education, advocacy and support, and promotes research.

https://www.tourette.ca

Life's a Twitch!

A Canadian website which provides information on Tourette syndrome and associated disorders. It is run by Dr B. Duncan McKinlay, who has Tourette syndrome himself.

www.lifesatwitch.com

www.cpri.ca/families/programs-services/brake-shop/brake-shop-virtual-clinic

Youthinmind Ltd

Provides information, assessment, treatment and research to promote psychological well-being.

http://youthinmind.info/py/yiminfo

Subject Index

Author Index

Uttom Chowdhury is a Consultant in Child and Adolescent Psychiatry at CAMHS Dunstable and a Visiting Professor in the Department of Applied Social Studies at the University of Bedfordshire. He is co-author of *Why Do You Do That?: A Book about Tourette Syndrome for Children and Young People*, also published by JKP, and is based in London, UK.

Tara Murphy is Consultant Clinical Psychologist and Paediatric Neuropsychologist at the Tic Disorder Clinic at Great Ormond Street Hospital. She has worked with children with tics and Tourette's for over twelve years and has published research and European guidelines on tic disorders. She is based in London, UK.

Printed in Great Britain
by Amazon